Healing Spiritual Amnesia

Healing
Spiritual
Amnesia

Remembering What It Means
to Be the Church

PAUL A. NIXON

Abingdon Press
Nashville

This book is printed on acid-free paper.

Library of Congress Cataloging-in-Publication Data

Nixon, Paul, 1962-
   Healing spiritual amnesia : remembering what it means to be the church / Paul Nixon.
     p. cm.
Includes bibliographical references.
   ISBN 0-687-06718-9 (alk. paper)
   1. Church growth.   I. Title.

BV653.25.N593 2004
262'.001'7—dc22

2003019361

04 05 06 07 08 09 10 11 12 13—10 9 8 7 6 5 4 3 2 1

MANUFACTURED IN THE UNITED STATES OF AMERICA

CONTENTS

PREFACE

Some years ago, I was a speaker at a conference of Methodists. As the meetings began, clergy and laity sat in anticipation, looking for some direction as to how they might revitalize their dying churches. People were aware that The United Methodist Church in the United States had been hemorrhaging members for years and that the annual reports revealed dramatic declines from coast to coast. Certainly there were exceptional churches that bucked the trend within this denomination, but, overall, the evidence was clear that the future did not look bright.

The bishop of this particular United Methodist Conference opened the meetings and, with a sarcastic smile, raised one fist in the air and shouted to the large assembly, "If the 1950s ever come back again, we're ready!"

The crowd laughed and applauded. The bishop had stated in that grand and humorous sentence all that was wrong and all that had to change if the churches of his denomination were to be effective agents of transformation in the twenty-first century. He had made clear that doing church as it was done in the 1950s will not cut it in the coming century. His message went on to declare that the survival of his denomination, and the growth of local churches as they reach out to the people in their communities, would be dependent upon the willingness to change and to adopt methodologies in styles of worship that communicate to the people who live in a new kind of world.

Adapting to the new sociological setting that churches now face does not mean abandoning the "old-time religion." In this book, Paul Nixon rightly points out that in years past the mainline denominations, attempting to be "relevant" to the emerging secularization process that was at work in the world around them, sought to secularize the gospel itself. They followed the lead of Friedrich Schleiermacher, the theologian who contended that the task of the church was to make the gospel meaningful to its "cultured despisers." In so doing, the followers of this trend cut the guts out of the Christian message and reduced it to a humanistic ethic with a high commitment to social justice values that they thought would be accepted by the society at large. Mainline denominations bought into this approach, and seminaries ended up with a couple of generations of preachers who knew how to talk about ways to achieve racial equality, military disarmament, gender equality, commitment to environmentalism, and overcoming poverty. But these same preachers, more often than we are ready to admit, lost the capacity to bring people into personal transforming relationships with Jesus Christ and to nurture their congregations into spiritual maturity through the disciplines of prayer and Bible study.

One should never get the impression that the social issues cited above are somehow inconsequential to the life of the Church or of secondary importance to those who call themselves followers of Jesus. But what has been missing in the sermons from too many mainline denominational pulpits is the declaration that for the church, commitments to such social justice issues must flow out of a deep commitment to Jesus Christ as Lord Savior and God. We need an emphasis on evangelism that calls people to a salvation that prepares them for heaven but primarily invites them to be surrendered to Jesus so that, through them, Christ might do his work in the world, transforming the world that is into the world that ought to be. John Wesley, the founder of Methodism, is a brilliant example that being mystically invaded by the Holy Spirit, and being deeply in love with a resurrected Christ, provides this kind of balance. Wesley called people to be filled with the Holy Spirit, which then motivated them to a commitment of overcoming the demonic effects of political oppression and economic deprivation. The Wesleyan revivals, according to the cultural historian Henry Steele Commager, brought about such dramatic social change in England that the likes of the French Revolution became unnecessary in order to correct prevailing social evils.

There is a tendency to forget that social change requires the transformation of individuals. If the Church can introduce its people to Christ and disciple them with solid biblical teachings, it will change them into persons with commitments to social justice. The best way to start a social movement is to have people so in tune with Christ that their hearts are breaking because there are things in the world around them that break his heart.

I wonder how many mainline seminary graduates, over the last year, have been able to lead anyone into a salvation experience. When I was in seminary, jokes were made about those who would reduce the gospel to what Bill Bright and Campus Crusade called "The Four Spiritual Laws." We mocked the *simplistic* gospel outlined in that tract. Often ignored was that an easy way to understand presentation of the gospel is where most people have to begin their spiritual journey.

The Scriptures introduce people to the mind of Christ. You cannot read through the pages of the Holy Book without becoming aware that our God has a heart for the poor. God is the liberator from oppression and calls the people of the Church to abolish poverty. But, too often, mainline preachers have embraced the mission prescribed by God and propagated it, without teaching from scripture the justice imperatives of scripture. This book takes note of the importance of having a solid biblical undergirding to the development of discipleship in the local church. Recently, I spoke at a gathering of the National Council of Churches, endeavoring to explain how mainline denominations could connect with the dynamistic evangelicalism that has become so much a part of the American scene. I picked up a copy of the resolutions that had just been passed by the assembly of delegates and pointed out that the resolutions were brilliantly worded and reflected the kinds of concerns that the Church should have in the context of our troubled world. I let the delegates know that as I read through them, I found no disagreement with anything that was said. But I then raised the question how these resolutions differed from a document that would emerge out of a group of moral secular humanists. I pointed out that there was no reference to scripture in anything that was written. I let it be known that everything that had been set forth in the document was based on values that emerge from the Bible, but nowhere was there any reference that would connect the Bible to what was written.

I said, "The people in the pews are looking for statements, coming from this august body, that will motivate them to do the work of God in the world, but there must be evidence that what is being called for is prescribed by scripture. People must believe that the justice issues for which they are working are biblically prescribed. This document should be rewritten, and on every issue there should be the quoting of scripture and interpretation of that scripture that provides the bases for the statements being made."

Churches in mainline denominations will not come back to life unless there is solid biblical study. We have allowed fundamentalists with a dispensationalist theology to steal the Bible from those of us who are in mainline denominations. We have not fed people the truths of scripture. When Karl Barth spoke at Princeton Theological Seminary, just before his death, he was asked by one of the students what was the greatest problem with theological education as it presently existed. Karl Barth answered, "If I asked the typical student in a mainline denominational seminary what Paul Tillich says about salvation, he could answer. If I asked what Emil Brunner says about salvation, I would get a good answer. If I asked the students what I believe about salvation, I believe that I could get a good answer.

However, if I asked what the apostle Paul specifically says about salvation, the response would be highly unsatisfactory. That is what's wrong with theological education in today's world."

Unless we train a generation of preachers who can say to the people from the pulpit, even as Billy Graham says from his pulpit, "The Bible says ...!" they will lack the authority that is required to call people to action.

What I especially enjoy about this book is that it is not designed simply to provide techniques to establish new megachurches. Of course there is a need for there to be new church plants that reach emerging communities across the country, and some of these churches, for sociological reasons, will grow into megachurches. This book goes beyond that and lays out themes whereby old established congregations that seemed doomed to extinction can be revitalized and become dynamic growing bodies of believers.

My mother once said, "It's less of a miracle to give birth than to resurrect the dead." She said that in reference to churches, and she was right. Resurrecting dead churches is one of the most difficult tasks that must be faced by mainline denominations, but this is the task that must be addressed if they are to survive. This book clearly sets forth ways to facilitate such resurrections. Churches that follow the scenarios prescribed here may not become megachurches (although some may), but they will probably become dynamic congregations with healthy ministries. What is more, these revitalized churches can offer something quite different from what can be experienced in the megachurches that are increasingly dotting the landscape.

Change will be required by these congregations. There will have to be changes in music and in programming. But it can be done, and it must be done. It must be done, not just because we want mainline denominations to survive, but because we believe that mainline denominations, with balanced theologies connected to great historical traditions, are desperately needed in today's world.

I live in Wayne, Pennsylvania, where a couple of decades ago a new church plant exploded on the scene. It drew into its fellowship hundreds and hundreds of people from the mainline churches that had been the mainstay of my community. Particularly hard hit was the Presbyterian church. Many people wondered what the future of this particular congregation would be in the face of this dynamic new congregation that featured contemporary worship, a solid social ministry to the poor, and a strong evangelical witness. Then the unexpected happened: As this dying congregation tried to reach back into its glorious past for an answer to their declining membership, they called as their pastor the son of a minister who had pastored the church during its glory days. Most of us assumed that this was the worst kind of wishful thinking; but we were wrong! The new preacher preached a solid evangelical message that got people to take Jesus seriously. He introduced a biblically based discipleship program and nurtured some of the old-timers of the church into a praying fellowship.

The results were astounding. The attendance at worship today is triple what it was just eight or nine years ago. People from the new megachurch who had come from this congregation have drifted back. Many have done so to reaffirm their identity as Presbyterians. Others have come back because they enjoy its traditional worship with organ-playing, robed choir, and so forth. It should be noted that this church has added a contemporary worship service on Saturday nights that draws in members of Generation X, along with some Boomers. Here is proof that a dying mainline congregation can come back to life and grow.

Today, the megachurch in my town, which hasn't lost any of its strength and dynamism, is alive and well. But alongside it is this equally strong Presbyterian congregation that offers to the people of Wayne a different kind of worship, with a strong emphasis on liturgy and a viable discipling program. Each of these churches has its niche. They live together in a mutually supportive fashion.

If you want to know all the details of how this mainline church pulled off its renewal and growth, then reading this book will give some answers. This book lays out exactly what has to be done for the dead bones of a fading congregation to take on new life and rise again.

Tony Campolo
Professor Emeritus
Eastern University
St. Davids, Pennsylvania

CHAPTER 1

ARE WE
FORGETTING
SOMETHING?

A mnesia is one of those wonders (or horrors) of nature that has long captured human imagination. Getting bonked on the head or witnessing a terrible trauma and then, in turn, losing memory of a certain span of time: This is amnesia. In worst cases, we may forget our identity altogether. Surely this ranks up there with quicksand and carnivorous fish in its sheer power over us, the power to erase us. Erasing memory is a partial erasing of our very existence. Our sense of identity is removed: In certain respects, *we cease to be,* albeit while we are yet alive.

Eleven months after the September 11, 2001, tragedy, a missing New Jersey man, presumed dead by many, was discovered in a New York health care facility. When he was reunited with his family, no one could say for sure where he had been on September 11. The man could not even remember his name. After several months of care, he remembered his birth date and part of his social security number, enough for authorities to piece together his identity. His family can only guess what horrors he may have witnessed on September 11. Amnesia had hidden those things from his mind, those and other key memories essential to his self-identity. He had been alive throughout the year 2002. But without his memory, his days were lived in total disconnect with his past. It was as if he had died, and another person now occupied his body.[1]

An old Methodist hymn begins by posing the question, "And are we yet alive?" It is a question of spiritual life (and death). It is a question that each church, each individual, each generation must regularly ask anew. As I scan the landscape of established Christian congregations in North America, almost everywhere I see some signs of spiritual life. Occasionally the life borders on vitality, especially outside the old denominational institutions. But in most places, I see life without a fully developed sense of Christian identity. I see spiritual amnesia, a vague cluelessness about who we are and what God has called us to be and do. In more than a few houses of worship, it is as if the church that used to live there has died and another family now lives in its house, claiming its name, wearing its clothes, and singing its favorite old songs.

Everywhere I Turn

In one place, I see a Sunday school class enjoying the works of William Faulkner as its main course of study, while its members remain blissfully ignorant of vast portions of the Bible. They delight in the exploration of exquisite thoughts. But the exploration is uncentered and unanchored.

In another place, I see a church board of trustees sitting on a mountain of funds, yet unwilling to perform urgently needed renovations on the church parish hall, unwilling, that is, until a well-heeled member books the room for his daughter's wedding reception. They are hesitant even to move the money to an account bearing higher interest without first conducting a six-month study. They are almost paralyzed at the thought of actually *parting* with the cash. They have forgotten why people gave all that money and why we have boards of trustees. They also seem to have forgotten why they once built a fellowship hall.

In several places, I see a head usher who no longer unlocks the front door of the sanctuary for worship, reasoning that all the members come in the side door instead. The usher has forgotten about the people who've never been inside the doors.

Down South, I see a church that still holds *revival* services, singing the praise and worship songs of the 1890s and 1920s in an alien land. They remember the forms of long ago, but they are now a hundred years detached from the explosive chain reaction of human life transformation that gave rise to the songs they sing. They remember the music of new birth, but they have long forgotten the power of new birth.

Out in suburbia, I see a relatively young church bursting at the seams, yet strangely unwilling to add more service times or to enlarge its worship space. The reasons vary. Some love the architecture of their present chapel. Others cherish the precious memories there. They came to the church because of the intimate family feel. They do not want to ruin the tight sense of community by making space in their life and facilities for others. When I see this particular church, satisfied simply with a full house, I am sad. For I know that their contentment provides the very reason their lovely chapel may be nearly empty a couple of generations from now. They have forgotten why we build chapels and sanctuaries.

I see an affluent church spending millions of dollars on itself and its institutional overhead, while throwing pennies at the suffering world around it. This church has forgotten Jesus' teaching about our responsibility to the poor.

I see a church of busy community leaders and responsible parents so distracted by endless commitments and personal over-scheduling that they don't really have time to think about the purpose and mission of the church. They are distracted by the business of living and leading at twenty-first-century speed. When we become as tired and as numb as many of the folk who worship alongside us each Sunday, it is easy enough to forget our first names and easier still to forget why we are a church.

Almost anywhere that I see a church trying to change its worship times or musical styles to reach new people, I see a corresponding uprising by certain members who feel well served by the present music and the present worship times. For many of these folks, there is no imaginable reason, no divine mission, that would justify such inconvenience to their Sunday habits. Somewhere along the way, they forgot.

I see plenty of youth ministries whose purpose is to entertain the children of church members with never-ending field trips and slumber parties. When asked why such entertainment is so important, the sponsors are quick to reply, "These activities keep the kids out of trouble." Keeping kids out of trouble: It seems like a decent enough mission, until we recall the mission Jesus gave us.

Within the historic North American denominations, I see more energy and focus revolving around the ideal of diversity than around any core principle that might form the basis of our unity. Missionally, this results in chaos and inertia.

In those churches that pride themselves for the ways they color outside the lines of dead convention and tradition, I sometimes see enthusiasm. However, a second look often leaves me wondering if it is really more enthusiasm for *enthusiasm* than enthusiasm for a meaningful, disciplined learning of our Savior's way of life. We are enthusiastic about enthusiasm, about clapping hands and upbeat rhythms. In short, many of us are more in love with emotional expression and *the fun of having church* than in love with Jesus. In such cases, our worship may be an outright party, but it often lacks grounding with the historical movement of God in human life as documented in Scripture and unfolded across the centuries.

In almost every established church, I see the tendency to get caught up in the mechanics and the routines. The longer the people in the church have known one another, the more often I see relational melodramas and histories among individuals, distracting them from the holy purposes for which God has called them together as a church.

In old churches and in young churches, in growing churches and in declining churches, in big churches and in small churches, in black churches and in white churches (and in all those in between), everywhere I look, I see *amnesia*—spiritual amnesia—spiritual life divorced from Christian memory and awkwardly connected, if at all, with the historic Christian mission.

Memory Is Precious!

Without memory, we quickly get lost. Memory is precious! Memory is the consciousness of our personal and community history, the archive of our experiences, the body of data that tells us who we are. We awaken each morning, and, within seconds, we recall not only who we are, but also what day it is and half the things we have planned to do that day. These things we have planned to do, they are memories—memories of plans made yesterday, plans rooted in where we are coming from. Memory helps us make decisions and choices that are in keeping with who we have been in the past. In this way, memory provides us with a set of signposts that make sense of the world, tell us right and wrong, and orient us for where we choose to go in life. When we lose memory, all the signposts are suddenly down. Without memory, we find ourselves on a highway with no signs, with no markers. And we get lost. It can be a terribly frightening experience, a nightmare, for both the person who loses memory and those who are forgotten.

If you have ever been caught in a blizzard in which visibility dropped, the road signs were hidden by blowing snow, and you could barely even see the road, you remember that you likely did not get home on time that evening. You may not have made it home at all. If you have ever tried to log off or on to a computer whose monitor has gone out, you know that the chances are remote that you will get where you want to go. It is almost impossible to move around purposefully on a computer's hard drive staring at a dark screen. Without the signposts on the monitor's screen that we all take for granted, we just peck away in the dark, hoping that we are not performing some inadvertent command that will erase our data.

Knowing where we have come from and what roads we have traveled to get here helps us know which roads we need to travel today and tomorrow. Memory links today with yesterday in a common river of identity.

What Is Amnesia?

Amnesia refers to a variety of conditions in which memory is lost and human beings lose touch with a chunk of time. The unaccounted gap in time may represent a few hours, a few days, or many years. Sometimes, the amnesia clears up within a few hours or days. Sometimes it remains for the rest of a person's life. Sometimes, amnesia comes with an inability to process new information or form new memories. Other times, amnesiac people seem to function normally except for lack of certain past memory.[2]

In most instances, amnesia is a stress- or trauma-induced condition. Brain injury, shock, fatigue, grief, fear, repression, illness—there are many possible events (both physical and psychological) that contribute to the onset of memory lapse in human beings. Occasionally, sixty years of memory are lost with no documented stress or physiological disorder associated. In these cases, the amnesia may be permanent, and its cause may remain a mystery.

Amnesia, as the medical community would think of it, refers to a disorder experienced within individual persons. In this book, I take the idea of amnesia and use it as a metaphor for the loss of memory within a spiritual community, specifically within the Christian community. Communities, like individuals, have memories. Communities, like individuals, can lose their memories through various stresses and traumas.

No metaphor is perfect. The parallels between amnesia diagnosed in psychiatric medicine and the kinds of amnesia we will consider in this book are not exact. Memory loss and dissociation have so many different causes. There is also no single pattern of memory recovery that can be generalized to all types of amnesia. And there remains much about amnesia that is yet a mystery to scientists.

But the experience of amnesia remains a powerful metaphor. Loss of memory profoundly disrupts life. It disconnects us with our past and, in so doing, damages our present and future as well.

Corporate memory is a bit different from individual memory. Individual memory, on the one hand, is housed primarily in the brain, enhanced by a diary here or a picture album there. Groups, on the other hand, have no common brain. A group's memory is often committed to writing, especially if the group has been around for more than a single generation. In ancient times, the memory of the group was encased in sacred stories told around the campfire over the course of many generations. Nevertheless, group memory is as important to a group's continued self-awareness and life effectiveness as individual memory. Without memory, a group will soon get lost.

The loss of memory in communities is usually related to some sort of stress introduced into the community's life. However, because the life of a group may be many times the length of an individual's life, the nature of the disturbance that interrupts corporate memory may be less sudden, more drawn out in time.

In the following pages, we will explore a few of the traumas that Christian communities experience that may contribute to memory loss. These traumas include changing cultural values, scandals, increasing exposure to non-Christian religions and ideologies, community exodus of a congregation's historic population groups, congregational or denominational conflicts, financial crises, the anesthetizing power of material wealth and affluence, the brain drain of highly competent potential pastors to other professions, suffocating control by overbearing individuals or factions within a congregation, and the accumulation of personal losses and grieving within a congregation, which causes members to look to their church primarily for comfort (rather than for mission). However, if I were to cook down to *one word* the trauma that is more related to our memory loss than any other thing, that word would be "change."

Change Is Traumatic

We are suffering from an unprecedented rate of change in our world, in our families, and in our spiritual communities. Perhaps you know the old joke about the boy who went to the store to get soap to wash his dog. He picked out the familiar laundry detergent that his family used. The cashier warned him to consider getting a pet shampoo instead, but the boy's mind was set on the laundry detergent. The next day, the boy wandered back into the store, looking dejected. The cashier saw him and asked, "It was the detergent, wasn't it? Something happened to your dog?" "Yes," said the boy, "my dog died. But I don't think it was the detergent that got him. I think it was the spin cycle." The spin cycle of the twenty-first century has thrust more change at the church in a shorter span of time than ever before. Most churches that are more than twenty years old are reeling from the spin cycle of social change; they are disoriented and losing touch not only with the world about them, but also with their own purpose and mission in that world.

Lovett Weems, director of the G. Douglass Lewis Center for Church Leadership at Wesley Theological Seminary in Washington., D.C., in a 2002 address to leaders of his denomination, reminds us all that organizations are created to resist change, not to embrace it easily.[3] Human organizations bring stability to the community by resisting change. Even with the Christian Church, one of its greatest services to Christ and to humanity has been to freeze our understanding of Jesus as the Son of God.

Sociologist Nancy Ammerman has studied hundreds of churches dealing with change in their communities, only to conclude that, all other factors being equal, when communities change, most churches can be counted on to respond to the stress of change by doing things the same way they have done them in the past. Weems likens it to a gravitational pull. Groups cling to constancy and stability like the moon to the earth.

Think about what change does to us. It knocks us silly. It throws us into shock. It disorients us. We, as communities, struggle to snap back from this shock by scrambling to remember who we are, to recover our wits, to claim our identity as best we can. The trouble is that we often rally around the wrong memories. Very often, when under stress, communities remember their historic forms and time-sensitive strategies, not their timeless mission and values. Form and strategy grow *out of* mission and values, not the other way around. Mission and values are about identity. Form and strategy are contextual applications of long-standing principles. Every good form and strategy is appropriate to certain situations. But when those situations change, form and strategy often need to change as well, guided by a stable sense of mission and values. When we respond to change by canonizing yesterday's structures and ministry strategies, we may inadvertently betray our original mission.

Baseball and Community Memory

For an example of how community memory works, let's step away for a moment from the world of faith communities to the world of sports. Let's consider the community of baseball. Baseball has been around about 150 years. For decades, it was a marginal interest and hobby within American society. However, with the advent of radio, millions of people, most of whom might never have entered a professional baseball stadium, were exposed to nightly baseball broadcasts. For a whole generation of Americans, the pleasure of summer evenings in the 1930s, 40s, and 50s was associated with baseball, broadcast from Chicago, St. Louis, Detroit, New York, and Atlanta. Artful wordsmiths such as Harry Carrey and Ernie Harwell painted pictures in the night, pictures of baseline drives and winning runs. There was something magical about it. On the evenings no game was broadcast, the radio listeners cleared vacant lots in their cities and on their farms and played baseball themselves. In the 1950s and 1960s, we watched the rise of Little League, as a new generation of children took up glove and bat. In the 1980s, T-ball became all the rage for preschoolers who did not have the motor skills to hit a moving ball. Millions of American children have now played T-ball and thereby been initiated into the community of baseball.

By the turn of the twenty-first century, baseball had a life of its own, a multigenerational community of people who (1) loved the sport, (2) knew the rules of the sport, (3) understood key strategies to play well, and (4) remembered extraordinary baseball players and records set across the decades.

To love baseball was to love the sounds, the tastes, and the smells of summertime. It was to love both the joy and the discipline of teamwork. It was to love the challenge of players rising to give their very best. It was often to love strategy and psychological intimidation as well.

In 1996, a Major League Baseball players' strike angered large numbers of baseball fans and caused them to give up watching baseball. By this time, the sport had become fully professionalized, with major business interests and even players investing in baseball as much for the enormous financial benefits as for the pure love of the game. In the wake of the strike, pundits prognosticated that baseball was no longer America's pastime. Yet, a couple of seasons after the strike, almost everyone who had ever loved baseball was back, and professional baseball teams were setting attendance records all across America. Our love affair with baseball persisted, despite the commercialization of the sport and despite the threat of another strike a few years later. Little League participation similarly reached new heights in its number of participants. Those who had at first feared the baseball strike would turn us off to baseball realized, by the late-1990s, that millions of Americans were as in love with baseball as ever.

However, despite the continued energy and money that spin around this sport, a tectonic shift has occurred over the past forty years. Baseball lost its innocence. It became big business. The strike was simply a symptom of a deeper and very significant change at the heart of what it means to play baseball. In the twenty-first century, no longer do we play ball on empty lots. Now we spend big money to suit up our seven-year-olds as if they played for the Dodgers. Now parents fill the stands, with ever-increasing thirst for winning. Now in the major leagues, a typical night for a family of three or four at the new high-tech ballparks might cost $200 or more. One of the reasons that so few people were truly bothered by the threat of another players' strike in 2002 is that so few baseball fans can remember when things were different. Memories of old-time baseball are rapidly passing away. Many would argue that a new game altogether is rapidly taking its place.

Baseball's greatest trauma has been the stampede from all quarters to cash in on the monetary potential of the sport. In the wake of this change, a significant and shrinking minority of fans protested. Most of us, however, found that forgetting was a much easier way of coping and dealing with such change.

John Eldridge, in his book *The Journey of Desire*, tells the parable of a sea lion beached in a desert terrain, far from any sea. For many years, the sea lion dreamed and longed for the sea, knowing that he was made for something far different from the place where he dwelled. However, in time, remembering the ocean became more painful than forgetting. After all, he lived in a desert. And he came to believe that he would always live in a desert. So he stopped dreaming of the sea. From sea lions to sports fans to whole nations: How often we discover great pain in the discrepancy between what is and what ought to be. Forgetting can be a self-prescribed form of pain management.

From Baseball to Spiritual Community

The parallels between the baseball community and the spiritual community are many and obvious. We each start with children. We each have our rules, our formative memories, our temples, and our evangelistic backup strategies for those we did not reach in childhood. We each put a lot of stock in star players. We each have our skeptical pundits who warn us that the sky is falling, and we each have demonstrated resiliency that almost always outlives these skeptics. We each contend with memory lapses, especially in the wake of change and stress.

The Christian community is, of course, much, much older than the community of baseball. Because of our linkage with the Hebrew community, we share in a continuous stream of group spiritual identity that goes back thousands of years. Throughout this long history, we have experienced regular lapses of memory, which usually have been corrected by one reformation or another. The history of the Hebrew people between 1300 B.C. and 500 B.C. is a continuous tale of spiritual forgetfulness, a cycle in which, on an almost generational basis, certain pagan influences kept creeping back into Hebrew worship only to be banished again by one prophetic movement after another.

At the comfortable distance from which we read the Old Testament, it may seem crazy, almost cartoon-like, how a people could be so forgetful as the Hebrew people were in the generations following the great deliverance from Egypt. How could a people forget so much so fast, when their very existence as a people was a result of a series of miracles?

With amnesia, be it in the individual or in a large group, the answer to the above puzzle is always the same. Amnesia occurs when it becomes *less painful* simply to forget than to juggle both the formative memories and the realities of the present. People rarely lose their identity casually, as if there were nothing better to do on a Saturday afternoon. There is always a reason.

As we saw above, baseball was assaulted by money. Over time, both its owners and its players saw in it the potential to become very, very rich. The faith of the early Hebrew people was similarly assaulted, assaulted in the following ways:

1. Their faith was assaulted by constant threats to their security from other tribes and peoples who lived around them. It is hard to live on a spiritual plane when you are constantly under attack from this tribe or that. It is hard to have church when you are constantly having war.

26

2. Their faith was assaulted by their wandering eyes.
Their young men were forever enraptured by the beautiful Middle Eastern women who lived about them.
These women belonged to other tribes and traditions, which did not worship the one God. Once individuals became entangled in relationships with people of radically different faith, religions quickly began to mix. Clarity and spiritual memory began to fade.

3. Their faith was assaulted by the quirky weather of Palestine. As the Hebrew people shifted from nomadic life to settled life, they began to farm and depend upon the rain. Of course, the rain in Palestine has never been predictable. It would be like trying to do agriculture in Southern California without irrigation. But the stakes were life and death. Talk about stress! Talk about pressure! How easy it was to borrow the superstitious habits of pagan farmers, whose various religious practices had evolved over the centuries as a way to cope with the weather by attempting to manipulate it.

Each time the Hebrews lost their identity and connection with their God, they would fall apart politically and militarily. Surrounding tribes would rout them, kill their sons, steal their daughters, and humiliate them. And then a prophet would rise up and tell it the way it was. They would turn back to God en masse. God would then restore their fortunes. That was the Old Testament cycle.

Spiritual Amnesia Did Not End in the Pre-Christian Era

The Christian community, which grew out of the first-century Jewish synagogue, today touches and embraces more than 1.5 billion living souls. These many people have vastly differing faith experiences and practices. However, it is safe to say that more than 1.5 billion persons are embraced, or at least vaguely claimed, by some Christian church somewhere.

Christian groups have no better record than their Hebrew forebears when it comes to the retention of spiritual memory. The
history of Christianity is a tale of forgetting and remembering.
The remarkable and hopeful reality is that we have a strong tradition of remembering, alongside our history of forgetting. We
must recognize that for every pastor, prophet, or renewal agent
today who rolls up his or her sleeves to seek to heal the amnesia,
there have been many more who labored before them and, by
God's grace, brought renewed spiritual identity and vitality to the
people. All ye who would be healers of spiritual amnesia, you
stand with a grand company of saints, whose efforts God has
blessed richly: Augustine, Benedict, Luther, Calvin, Menno
Simons, Schleiermacher, William Seymour, and Barth.

When one Christian group loses its identity or forgets significant aspects of its roots, there is almost always another rising to
fill the gap and remind us who we are. When the world as we
knew it was collapsing with the old Roman Empire, and the
Christian movement with it, Augustine of Hippo rallied us to
remember who we were. When we, in our tedious doctrine and
immense political power, had lost touch with piety, Benedict rallied us to remember. When Roman Catholicism was later
embroiled in scandal and pettiness, several strands of Protestant
Christianity emerged, reaffirming key truths that had been forgotten in one way or another. When, later, many groups of
Protestants became so enamored with enlightenment thinking
that their belief in the supernatural all but dried up, William
Seymour showed up at 312 Azusa Street in downtown Los
Angeles, preaching the baptism of the Holy Ghost, rekindling a
first-century spirit in a worldwide Christian community that had
become tired, sleepy, and institutional.

I look at Christianity as a whole and marvel at its vitality,
twenty centuries after the Christ event. The Christian movement continues to demonstrate a remarkable resiliency and
capacity for renewal. This is certainly a sign that God's Spirit
continues to create life within the Church.

And yet, even where there is renewal of doctrine and method,
spiritual amnesia persistently and quickly returns. Even where

Bibles are systematically studied, spiritual amnesia often stubbornly persists. In denominations and congregations that have been around for more than a couple of generations, the current lack of spiritual memory is staggering. Both in North America and in Europe, we are closing down ministry sites faster than we are adding new sites. Within many Christian groups, we are drifting into syncretism, a mixing of Christian themes with symbols and truths arising from non-Christian world religions, creating new faith traditions altogether, much like the biblical Samaritans once did.

And of course there is one huge difference between a sports community and the Christian community: The latter was created by God. We may wring our hands at the loss of old-fashioned baseball. But it is fair to say that the stakes are infinitely greater when we consider the loss of vital Christian community.

Four Types of Spiritual Amnesia

Amnesia often looks different in one place than in another. In fact, it may be helpful for us to think about spiritual amnesia as a fourfold phenomenon. Few spiritual communities experience the amnesia on all four levels. A few do. A few others possess a strong identity in all four arenas and suffer from no amnesia at all. Most churches seem to be somewhere in the middle, experiencing amnesia in at least one of the four arenas.

These four main manifestations of spiritual amnesia are as follows:

- Forgetting who Jesus is.
- Forgetting the holy habits or spiritual disciplines, which mark us as belonging to Jesus.
- Forgetting our neighbor.
- Forgetting how to be effective in reaching our world. (This is tricky, since the technology is always changing.)

As I work with congregations, I often find it helpful to pause and mentally run through the four amnesias and to ask, "What are we forgetting here?" Especially for a church that seems stagnated or "stuck" and is genuinely puzzled as to what the trouble is, naming the amnesia seems to cast light on a whole host of mysteries. Naming the amnesia also helps us focus our conversation on the most critical issues in that place.

In the pages that follow, we will examine each form of spiritual amnesia, looking at the traumas and stresses that often give rise to them. However, the most important part of this exploration is the discovery of ways that spiritual memory can be recovered. This is primarily a book about how we can access *the healing* God desires for us.

If God Has Not Yet Given Up on Established Churches, Who Are We to Give Up?

There are many Christian leaders, our best and brightest, who are giving up on the difficult task of trying to lead established churches to accomplish their mission. In many cases, these men and women are choosing instead to plant new communities, discovering freedom to minister apart from stifling traditions and controllers. It is almost a cliché among transformational pastors (after an exhausting turnaround experience of a long-established, previously declining church) that "if I had it to do over again, I would just go and start a church from scratch rather than try to lead an established church to embrace authentic mission." Successful leadership of established congregations usually entails a fight of some kind. Wise leaders try to keep this struggle focused in manageable arenas and to count carefully the cost of any and every potential battle. Jesus, himself, knew something about this principle firsthand.

Let me be very clear: We need new churches! Helping start churches is what I do for a living! There is little doubt in my mind that pastors who are wired to reach secular and non-church-culture people will usually reach more people by starting from scratch than by assuming leadership of established congregations and spending valuable energy fighting the controllers of the status quo in those congregations.

And yet, I am troubled by the notion that most of the churches we plant in the next twenty years will slowly become dysfunctional and detached from their identities. How tragic the thought that Christian groups and congregations are destined to be lost to their mission after the first twenty years of their existence! This idea negates the gifts and potential of hundreds of millions of people whose lives are invested in the ministry of established Christian communities.

I believe there is another way, a way of healing, that does not sap the precious energy of God's people in endless conflict. Congregations can, in fact, find spiritual healing through recovered memory. In the words of Jeff Shaara, from the preface of his father's novel *For Love of the Game*, "The wounds heal and the memories return."[4]

This book represents the efforts of one man to tend to some old wounds, so that we can reestablish and fortify the holy memories that are critical to the future of the Christian movement. The following pages are offered in the belief that leadership toward church revitalization will more likely succeed once we have addressed the amnesias present in a congregation and sought God's healing.

Study Questions

1. Have you ever known a person who suffered from memory loss? If so, how did his or her family deal with this loss of memory? Was there a sense in which the person suffering from the loss of memory had also been lost?

2. How do you feel about the author's premise that many churches also suffer from memory loss? Do you agree? Do you disagree? Why? Or are you unsure?

3. Can you see a connection between stress and memory loss in your church? Share your observations with the group.

4. Do you thrive on change personally, or do you feel yourself on change overload? What about your church: Does it thrive on change or resist change?

5. Without having read in full how the author will define and explain the four types of amnesia, which type(s), if any, do you feel may be present in the life of your church. Why do you feel this way? What evidences do you see?

6. Do you feel that spiritual amnesia is curable? Or does this topic overwhelm you and make you not want to pick up this book again?

7. What are your hopes and prayers as you and your group study this book? Be as specific as possible. Close with a prayer time committing these things to God.

Notes

1. Richard Lezin Jones, "Long After 9/11, a Missing Man Turns Up in a Manhattan Hospital," *The New York Times on the Web*, 28 August 2002.

2. Sources helpful to me in learning about amnesia include *Textbook of Psychiatry*, 3rd ed., ed. Robert E. Hales, M.D., Stuart C. Yudofsky, M.D., and John Talbott, M.D. (Washington, D.C.: The American Psychiatric Press, 1999); *The Merck Manual—Home Edition*, sec. 7, chapter 90, "Dissociative Disorders"; and the following journals: *American Journal of Psychiatry*, *Arch Neurol*, and *The Lancet*. My thanks to Ed Mobley, M.D., Psychiatrist and Director of the Medical Staff at Baptist Medical Center in Pensacola, Florida, for connecting me to several of these sources and for teaching me about amnesia over the course of several conversations in the summer and fall of 2002.

3. Lovett Weems, "Leading the 21st-century Church" (keynote address of The School of Congregational Development, sponsored by The General Board of Global Ministries and The General Board of Discipleship of The United Methodist Church, August 1, 2002).

4. Michael Shaara, *For Love of the Game* (Hampton Falls, N.H.: Thomas T. Beeler, 1991), 2.

CHAPTER 2

REMEMBERING
WHO JESUS IS

"I am the way, and the truth, and the life. No one comes to the Father except through me." John 14:6

A Tale of Two Churches

Trinity Church and Grace Church have shared the corner of Eighth and Pecan for as long as any member at either church can remember. They are of two different denominations, and their sanctuaries are located on opposite corners of a major intersection in a midsized Midwestern American city. For years, Trinity Church was slightly larger than Grace Church and slightly more affluent. Both churches have a strong history of community leadership as well as leadership within their respective denominational families. They also have a strong history of friendly competition, completing their respective sanctuaries, education annexes, and family life centers within only a few months of the other. Over the decades, the two churches have cross-pollinated. Families intermarried between the two churches. Children attended church camp and vacation Bible school freely at both churches. The community Thanksgiving service and high school baccalaureate service still flip-flop back and forth across the intersection. Trinity and Grace have the two largest sanctuaries in the county, the only rooms large enough to hold the baccalaureate crowd. The Thanksgiving service is not nearly as large today as twenty years ago, but tradition keeps it at either Trinity or Grace each year.

In recent years, Trinity Church's parking lot typically collected fewer cars than in Sundays past, though Grace Church continued to pack in as many as ever. In fact, judging from life on the street and in the parking lot, Grace appeared to be substantially larger and younger than the Trinity congregation. The people at Trinity were puzzled by this, wondering why they had "lost the young people" during a period when Grace attracted a large new contingency of young adults and children, some of whom have family history over at Trinity. This question lingered on the minds of the Trinity people, while the people at Grace were so busy that most never stopped to notice the emptier parking lot at Trinity.

A Tale of Divergent Choices

Granted, in recent years, Grace and Trinity have made some very different choices. In the last round of sanctuary renovations, Grace added a rear projection video screen and sound system while Trinity enlarged their pipe organ. Grace received a new pastor a few years back who had not graduated from seminary, a first in the church's history. Trinity selected a new pastor the very same year, one who had excellent pedigrees and regularly lectured at prestigious East Coast clergy events. A few weeks after arrival, Trinity's new pastor read one of those lectures as the Sunday sermon. Finally, Grace began a ministry to homeless and indigent persons *independent* of the social ministry efforts put forth by the joint community of churches. Trinity responded to this news by increasing its financial pledge to the ecumenical ministry, even though few of its members regularly volunteered there anymore. One weekend, Grace brought in a Grammy Award–winning Christian musician and packed their house with 700 people at $20 a seat. The next night, across the street at the Trinity Chancel Choir cantata, complete with two selections in Latin, fewer than 150 people attended, even though admission was absolutely free.

The above choices directly affected Grace and Trinity. These two churches were once separated only by minor nuances of polity and liturgy. More recently, however, the two seemed to have less in common than ever before. On the surface, we see simply different choices. But looking beneath the surface, we see a growing difference between the pastors of Grace and Trinity that is quite profound.

Looking Deeper

Two decades had passed since Trinity Church had a pastor who, in some meaningful sense, thought of Jesus as the *unique* Son of God who (1) died for the sins of the world, (2) came back to life on the first Easter, and (3) still transforms human life today. Twenty years. This news would have come as a surprise to some of the members at Trinity. But since Jesus has seldom ever been the talk of Trinity Church, it was easy to miss this significant change in their leader's relationship to (and beliefs about) Jesus.

The short irony was basically this: Regardless of what he said or didn't say, the pastor of Trinity no longer was trinitarian in his *experience* of God. Now he certainly believed in God. He even believed in miracles, at least in theory. When it came to Jesus, he knew all the stories, but that was it. He knew *about* Jesus, *all* about Jesus. But he did not know Jesus as a friend.

When the pastor's ordination committee grilled him on Christology a decade earlier, he gave a confident and intelligent answer about Jesus being a symbol of God's love for us. He threw in a few key words that would appease the wide range of theological beliefs in the room. He had a way with words that made everyone feel good. No red flags. No worrisome opinions. No heresy here. But the ordination committee missed one salient fact: This erudite and gracious man never spoke of a personal relationship with Jesus Christ. Trinity's new pastor definitely saw Jesus as a symbol of God's love, but he was unclear how or if Jesus ever *did* anything himself to make human salvation possible. It is not simply that the old atonement paradigms made no sense to him. *Trinity's pastor had no new atonement paradigm either, no working model of how Jesus' death and resurrection functioned to save people from sin and death.* And therein was trouble. He had no clear understanding of how persons could move from darkness to light by knowing and trusting Jesus. For this good man, Jesus was simply a very good teacher, a window to God's love, whose truth could also be accessed through certain non-Christian traditions.

Some Things We Don't Talk About

Over the last twenty years, the teaching and activities program at Trinity turned toward personal development and social justice, safe topics for an increasingly diverse congregation. Over this same period of time, Trinity slowly accumulated members who felt comfortable at Trinity precisely because of the stuff that did not get talked about. If one or two at Trinity were to raise a divisive doctrinal issue, it might create a conflict. A good brouhaha on Christology might splinter the congregation. In short, no one at Trinity was *about* to go there. Best leave Jesus alone.

Across the street at Grace Church, not only did their pastor talk about Jesus, but also he admonished the people to bring friends to church with them so that they too could meet Jesus. At Grace Church, they talked a lot about meeting Jesus, accepting Jesus, trusting Jesus, receiving Jesus, following Jesus. In short, Jesus was a big deal at Grace.

The members of Grace were encouraged to talk about their experience with Jesus, to share it with one another and with people beyond their fellowship. Across the street, most members of Trinity would have felt embarrassed to talk about so intimate a thing. And so with no one talking, no one really knew what anyone at Trinity was really thinking or believing. In fact, more than a few at Trinity would have been scared to know. And so a conspiracy of silence settled in at Trinity. They would talk about the weather. They would talk about their church building. They would talk about their travels. They would talk about their next potluck social. But never, ever did they talk about their personal experience with Jesus. And no one could remember the last time anybody *got saved* there, from anything.

So Where's the Trauma?

You may be thinking, "If amnesia is memory loss due to stress and trauma, where is the trauma in Trinity's story?" It is a good question. Despite a few controlling and overbearing personalities, the members at Trinity learned how to get along well. Perhaps too well. Trinity has no history of fighting or pouting or power struggles or harsh words. To the casual observer it may have seemed like a slow easy drift, like a sailboat whose anchor pulls loose during the night.

But there *are* reasons that three loving and highly educated pastors at Trinity drifted away from a classical Christian understanding of who Jesus is. Each loved God and possessed some sense that God had called him or her to care for God's people. So it was not for lack of loving God that they forgot who Jesus was.

Each of Trinity's last three pastors had left behind more lucrative career possibilities in other fields in order to attend seminary and seek ordination. So it was not for lack of commitment that they forgot who Jesus was.

One of the three pastors, in college, experienced an emotional and life-changing point of decision one summer evening. At least in her case, it was not for lack of a spiritual conversion experience that she forgot who Jesus was.

So what was it that happened? What caused Jesus Christ to slip in their minds from being a real person to being simply a metaphor? The answer: Each of the pastors was assaulted. Trinity's pastors were assaulted by a radically rationalistic world-view that is often at odds with the mystery and wonder of God. Every pastor in the history of Trinity Church has been a graduate of the same theological seminary. Now, I would quickly add that *nobody at the seminary meant to assault anybody*, except maybe for one crusty old professor who seemed to get his kicks from making his students squirm. But, save this rare exception, the pastors and professors who made up the education and credentialing system each meant well. Nonetheless, the road to hell is sometimes paved with the best of intentions.

Over the last thirty years, as the faculty at the seminary turned over, several of the new professors approached the Christian faith (and everything else in life) with the scientific skepticism that was the mark of modernity. More than a few of them seemed to have an ax to grind against the grassroots spiritual, social, and political instincts of the people in the parish. One professor regularly went into a polite tirade on how the idea of Jesus' blood paying for the world's sins reflected a cruel and primitive view of God. Another professor developed an entire lecture around the subject of the hymn "In the Garden" and how it is the worst hymn ever written. The whole idea of a person "walking and talking with Jesus" was deemed too sentimental and overpersonalized. In all fairness, we should note that the seminary has recently sought to counterbalance this trend with a renewed focus on personal spiritual formation. In fact, the faculty is probably more balanced at the seminary today than it has been for years. However, Trinity's pastors are now long out of seminary and unable to benefit from this mini-renaissance.

To read their student journals is to see that their theological formation was not always a gentle process. It sometimes posed a rather brisk assault on the faith they brought with them to school. One of the three argued once in class with what was being taught (by the crusty, inflammatory professor mentioned above). In turn, he was derided publicly. This was not the norm, however. The other two drifted into ambiguity quietly, possessing neither the tools nor the mentors to help them integrate faith with their learning. All three finally entered their pastoral work believing that the biblical portraits of Jesus were largely nonhistorical myths. All three left their seminary believing, mistakenly, that the world was becoming increasingly secularized and that the key to making the Christian faith relevant to contemporary people was to be as secular as possible themselves. All three had been taught to look within the Scriptures for universal principles that can be applied to either the betterment of society or the betterment of one's own mental and relational health.

The only place some mystery had been left intact for these students was in the area of worship and liturgy. There, students were encouraged to form an enchantment with certain repetitive rituals that made little sense to everyday people. However, as their inward faith had become more tenuous, they needed to find a stable center somewhere. Liturgical ritual offered this stability. In summary, Trinity's pastors graduated into parish ministry with dual instincts: to be as rationalistic as possible in terms of the Bible and to be as medieval as possible in terms of liturgy.

All three lacked a compelling motivation for engaging in evangelism. And for lack of such a motivation, why make the changes and innovations necessary to reach new generations and populations with the faith? The pastors of Trinity Church chose instead simply to love their flock. Trinity's creativity turned inward. The flock chose to use their creativity on projects and events that enhanced fellowship or entertained the mind. Enormous resources went into music and visual arts as defined by the educated elite who were increasingly chosen for leadership at Trinity.

Paralleling the assault of rationalism on the faith of the pastors, a good number of Trinity's members were immersed in professional degree programs of their own during their young adult years. These programs were part of the same Western educational model of the late twentieth century that was highly suspicious of all things having to do with God or faith. Many of them, too, graduated with a faith in disarray. And again, their church was unable to provide them with tools to integrate classical Christian faith with their education and their encounter with alternative worldviews.

Please do not hear this as an attempt to discredit the contemporary enterprise of higher education and theological training. I personally experienced a balance of academic rigor and faith in my college and seminary faculty. I have always felt that the academy was my friend in life and in ministry. But I talk to a lot of people who had a very different experience. Higher education is *not* the villain in this story. But we must recognize that higher education often provides a setting in which, at times, the left sphere of the human brain is allowed (or encouraged) to run amuck. The left sphere of the brain is all about logic and order and reason and proof. Rationalism is often simply "left brain out of control!"

I am not advocating a fundamentalist approach to theological education that attempts to freeze thought by providing a detailed compendium of doctrinal statements that are not subject to exploration and questioning. I am, however, advocating that we take great care to send our pastoral students to places of education and training where the professors can articulate their personal experience of salvation relative to Jesus Christ. Either we are comfortable with the assertion that Jesus saves people or we aren't. There is plenty of room in the church for people who struggle with classical Christology. I have gladly made space for many such people in the churches I have served as pastor. This is not to say, however, that such folks should be training Christian pastors.

Healing from the Assault of Rationalism

If we approach the Christian faith simply from the left side of the brain, we may end up with many questions and hesitations and without many conclusions or much passion. This is why the apostle Paul, at the beginning of his first letter to the church at Corinth, said,

> For the message of the cross is foolishness to those who are perishing. . . . Where is the wise man? Where is the scholar? Where is the philosopher of this age? Has not God made foolish the wisdom of the world? . . . For the foolishness of God is wiser than man's wisdom, and the weakness of God is stronger than man's strength. (1 Cor. 1:18*a*, 20, 25 NIV)

Go to a symphony. Watch a sunrise. Sit on the second row of a Spirit-filled black church. Hold your newborn baby, for goodness' sake. There is nothing logical about the feelings you will receive in any of these experiences. But there is much that is beautiful! Healing from the assault of rationalism very often will involve a powerful experience that taps the right sphere of our brain.

I was raised in a Christian home, in a pastor's home at that. We went to church three times a week. I've been at church since I was two weeks old. I didn't even take time out during college. My parents were good people, not prone to outward religious demonstration at home, but solid in their faith convictions and in the disciplines that grew from those convictions. In other words, their faith came home with them from church. My parents genuinely loved me, and they became my cheerleaders, encouraging me and energizing me across the years to go and do good things. At our house, there usually wasn't much money left by the end of the month, but my parents always provided something good to eat, something nice to wear, a comfortable place to call home, and the best schooling available. I was blessed. Only a tiny fraction of children who enter this world can claim all that I have just recounted in this paragraph.

But I haven't yet told you about the greatest gift of my childhood. Better than my parents' faith, better than receiving my parents' blessing, the greatest gift was this thing that happened to our church in 1972. This wild and wonderful thing. I was ten years old. And the thing continued until I was around fourteen. To this day, I do not understand what exactly happened.

I remember this. All the people around me began singing with a passion they never had before. My dad began preaching with a passion he had not had before. And one by one, people began experiencing life transformation like no one in that church had ever seen before. Darkness-to-light kind of stuff. Then they began adding metal folding chairs up and down the aisles and overflowing the choir loft. They added another service, then a larger building. And one Sunday night, at the end of a two-hour celebration of faith, I remember my dad saying with tears in his eyes, "When we are old men with long white beards, we will still remember what the Lord did in this place with this people." It's been thirty years now since that revival, or whatever it was that happened at Magnolia Avenue Baptist Church in Riverside, California, fifty miles east of Azusa Street. Yet that experience is still forming me spiritually.

When I went to college, I spent three solid years, day and night, in the library reading hundreds of books. I believe that I received more education in the university library than in any of the classrooms. Many, if not most, of the books I read challenged the faith worldview that I brought with me from my youthful encounter with the Holy. I felt a bit alone in those days. No one in the early 1980s was talking about what it meant to be postmodern. Many of us early postmoderns felt that we were the only ones on earth who thought and felt the way we did. I graduated from college certain that Josh McDowell, C. S. Lewis, and others had failed in their left-brain attempts to prove anything to me. I also left more deeply in love with Jesus than when I started. Less convinced than ever, and more in love than ever. What I was discovering in those early years was that the heart has reasons that reason doesn't know. All argument aside, I kept remembering the experience of meeting Jesus alive in all those people in Riverside. I did not know at age twenty-two how it would all finally fit together for me. But I knew this much: When logic tells me one thing and experience tells me another, I will go with experience every time. I think that is what it means to be a postmodern person. And I think this is what it meant to be a first-century Christian.

The Reasons That Reason Doesn't Know

Blaise Pascal not only is one of the great mathematicians of history, but also stands as one of the great Apologists (or defenders of the Christian faith) of the last millennium. Albert Einstein considered him the all-around most brilliant guy of the same thousand years; and coming from Einstein, that is no small honor. Pascal understood that rationalism was ultimately limited in its ability to apprehend reality. In his famous *Pensées*, he wrote, "Reason's last step is the recognition that there are an infinite number of things which are beyond it."[1] He went on to add the now famous words, "The heart has its reasons of which reason knows nothing. It is the heart that perceives God and not the reason."

However, the most remarkable words that came from Pascal's pen were never published in his lifetime. Eight years after his death, a worn parchment was discovered sewn into his coat, containing two copies of a personal statement that contained the following:

> The year of grace 1654. Monday, 23 November, feast of Saint Clement. . . . From about half-past ten in the evening until about half-midnight. Fire. The God of Abraham, the God of Isaac, the God of Jacob. Not of the philosophers and intellectuals. Certitude, certitude, feeling, joy, peace. . . . Joy, joy, joy, tears of Joy. . . . This is eternal life that they may know you, the one true God, and Jesus Christ whom you have sent. Jesus Christ. Jesus Christ.

Pascal had apparently sewn it into his coat so that he would see it daily, so that he would not lose touch with this reality that had become the foundation of his life, a reality that was, first of all, an *experience*. Theological ideas arose from the experience to be sure, but the foundation of Pascal's faith was revealed by his coat lining to be a personal experience of the holy, an experience of the living God. The New Testament faith came to us in exactly the same progression. From the powerful experience of the Christ event, there flowed new assumptions and earth-shattering truths. Wrested from their root in the experience of knowing Jesus and meeting him alive again beyond his execution, the truths of the Christian faith would have withered and the whole movement been stillborn. Just as a plant wrested from its soil will wither within hours, the Christian faith, pulled apart from a rooting in the kind of experience Pascal described above, will fade to mush and vapor in less than a generation's time.

The secular, *modern* way of looking at the world begins with two assumptions. The first assumption is that every event of any spiritual significance in the Bible or in our lives can be understood as a sequence of natural occurrences. Second, even if supernatural events are possible in theory, there is no hard proof that demands our assent.

It should be noted that the majority of human beings do not begin with these assumptions about the world. A few years back, while I was visiting Vancouver, British Columbia, supposedly one of the most secular cities in North America, I picked up a local newspaper. To my amusement and amazement, I discovered in the classified section of that paper scores of ads for all kinds of supernatural answers to life's challenges, everything from tarot cards to channelling. Many assume that in the twenty-first century, the people in "secular" cities are actually secular. A bad assumption. A few are, but not the masses. Not even in university communities. Look and listen closely and you will see. After all these many years, we human beings are still, at our deepest core, a people of the heart.

When we move from the playing field of logic and rationalism and shift over to the playing field of experience, we move to a setting in which we have the opportunity to discover and remember who Jesus is—by meeting him. For many individuals, this experience of Jesus happens in the context of loving relationships and impassioned worship in a church that knows Jesus. But if our church only knows about Jesus, and has little experience with him in terms of personal relationship, then going to church is not going to help us necessarily.

Healing comes by experience. The good people of Trinity Church did not feel free to talk about their experience of Jesus or their personal relationship with God through Jesus. This kind of conversation was outside their comfort zone and, for many of them, outside their personal experience. And so Trinity was gradually forgetting. The connections were loosening. The fragile memories were fading. Over at Grace Church, one salient difference over the last twenty years was a continued affirmation and nurturing of *experience*. Because of this, Grace Church recently shifted to more emotionally stirring music in its worship services. In addition, Grace continues to emphasize the importance of experiencing God's love personally, one life at a time. In these ways, Grace Church continues to expose people to reasons that reason does not know.

Misguided Zeal

Over the last century, particularly in the last couple of decades, as many denominational families have found themselves on the path toward becoming like Trinity Church in many ways, countermovements have arisen to pull the group back toward another vision, a vision more akin to Grace Church. These countermovements have often begun by describing the common beliefs and practices of churches such as Grace and then declaring such beliefs and practices as normative for their denominations. This has usually resulted in political struggle and polarization. It has divided brother against brother and sister against sister.

In these various holy wars, nobody really wins. The people on the Trinity side of the aisle usually come away even more alienated from behaviors that are key to remembering their mission. They end up more out of touch than ever. The people on the Grace side sometimes oversimplify the differences, draw lots of lines in the sand, and inadvertently cut themselves off from the valuable gifts and leadership offered by some of the Trinity folk. To my knowledge, there is no documented widespread spiritual awakening that has ever flowed out of one of these holy wars.

Often those who have given their lives to such battles have awakened after many hard-fought years to discover that their own adult children are utterly unable to see the same issues in black and white. After a quarter century of intense theological wrangling in many American denominations, many of our children refuse to confine themselves to this corner or that, or to label themselves according to 1980s-era divisions. We just fought a war, and now our kids don't care. Many thriving congregations of today's young adults are, theologically, a blending of Grace *and* Trinity, though their worship may resemble neither.

But the one common denominator in nearly every thriving twenty-first-century church, young and old, is that the believers come together to experience God, not simply to talk about him or to sing about him.

An Alternative to Holy War

An experience of the living God enables people to transcend their diversity and to escape polarization. Is this not one of the great lessons of Pentecost? When the Spirit of God came upon the believers, the experience spilled out of the gathering place into the streets and affected thousands of folks, bridging many languages and pulling diverse people into a unity.

In more recent years, the Pentecostal movement has been one of the answers to the powerful human craving for an experience of the Holy. Pentecostalism cuts across diverse doctrinal differences. Within some denominations, Pentecostal Christians have received a bad rap in the last quarter century. They've often been diagnosed, unfairly, as the troublemakers. Though it is possible for people of any theological tradition to be troublemakers, I think we must recognize that the people who find themselves in conflict with Pentecostals are often the same people who find themselves in conflict with "liberals" or "evangelicals" or any others whose experience of God and human life has broadened their outlook and their tolerance of sisters and brothers who express their faith differently. Modern Pentecostalism, in its various manifestations and movements, has almost always arisen and thrived in response to a legitimate need, a need that many churches do not adequately address. The need is for an experience of God. The lack of a fresh experience of God's presence is a gaping hole in many Christian communities. Though I have never been a part of a Pentecostal congregation, I share with Harvard theologian Harvey Cox a deep respect for the fundamental integrity and validity of any movement that has helped half a billion people meet Jesus.[2]

If a group of people gather together and their shared experience of God is sufficiently powerful, the slight differences in their interpretations of the experience are of lesser importance. Indeed, if their common experience is sufficiently powerful, the differences in their interpretations of that experience will be minor most of the time anyway. If, however, a second group of people gathers and there is little power in their common experience, the second group will, by necessity, depend more upon a common interpretation of truth, since their experience itself is too weak to unify them. Thus, as our experience of God wanes in power, our dependency upon creeds and confessional tests of orthodoxy often rises. The generation of Christians closest to Jesus worked with a simple creed because they were so close to the Christ event historically. Their faith was more about a life-changing experience than about a bunch of things they were supposed to believe. Throughout history, the rediscovery of Jesus has been accompanied by more often a simplifying of our doctrinal laundry lists than a lengthening of such lists.

Likewise, I would maintain that the best prescription for renewing our memory of Jesus is not a tightening of our creedal litmus tests. Rather, our best chance at widespread rediscovery of Jesus lies simply in meeting Jesus, all over again, encountering his Spirit in the here and now.

Trinity Church Meets Jesus Again

No one is sure when the turning point came for Trinity. There was really no single incident, but rather a series of events that deeply affected the heart and life of the Trinity congregation. First, there was a group of older women who began to pray for Trinity. Their agenda in coming together, at first, was that Trinity reconnect with "the young people," people under the age of forty who were the ages of their own children and who were increasingly missing from the life and worship of Trinity Church. Second, their latest pastor was diagnosed with a rare form of cancer and began experimental treatments. With his long-term life expectancy in jeopardy, he let go of his dream to teach at the seminary and began to ask how his life could make a difference day by day, in the place he was planted. Finally, a twelve-year-old girl in the Trinity congregation had been gifted with the voice of an angel. One Sunday she sang "The Lord's Prayer," and several people in the room were moved to tears. She began to sing regularly in the services, and whenever she sang, people almost leaned forward with expectation of a blessing. These three variables, which no church council or strategic planning committee could ever have engineered, came together and formed a spiritual whirlwind. Things began to happen that had not happened at Trinity for a long time.

One Sunday, several weeks into his cancer treatments, the pastor left his manuscript on the pulpit and walked among the congregation, sharing both his fears and his hopes. As he shared, he reached out and took the hand of a man sitting along the aisle, and then he took the hand of the woman seated in the next row. Then he began to weep. A sixteen-year-old boy arose and walked toward the pastor to place a hand on his shoulder. Then they began to rise all across the house. They surrounded him in a silent embrace of love. And then someone in the middle of the mob began to pray, followed by another, and then another. The worship service at Trinity had officially gone off script for the first time in anyone's memory. And it was, without doubt, the most wonder-filled moment that any of them could ever recall at church.

Six months later, Trinity's pastor was stronger and healthier than ever. He was also meeting people at the altar with oil in hand to anoint them and pray for their healing. During the preceding months, he had come to read the Gospel tales of Jesus' healing ministry through entirely different eyes. No longer did he read these stories simply as mythological tales to be given spiritual meanings when they came up in the lectionary rotation of scripture readings for worship. He now read them as real stories of God's grace poured out upon actual human lives, even as he had now experienced such grace. He began to rethink everything he had believed and disbelieved.

New faces began to appear each week at Trinity. Outwardly, they at first looked much like the folks who had attended Trinity for years, though this would change in time. But inwardly, they brought with them much sorrow, much illness, much brokenness, and much addiction. They came to find healing, to find power for new beginnings. As a community of persons who had received healing began to accumulate both within the Trinity fellowship and around it, the whole atmosphere at Trinity changed. Without any prompting by pastor or evangelism committee, the people of Trinity began to look for the new faces each week and to celebrate their presence and to pray that they might discover the healing touch of God.

The old women kept praying, but in time, their prayers were joined by many others. In fact, attendance at the midweek prayer service grew to encompass more than 150 people. And the little girl kept singing, along with many others who discovered a new song in their hearts. For several months, the best music was at the midweek prayer service, at which the director of music ministry exercised less control. However, in time, the music of Wednesday began to invade Sunday, and they all sang with a sense of soul and conviction (and rhythm) never before known at Trinity.

Finally, let it be noted, that several people over at Grace began to wonder what was going on over at Trinity. Grace finally dispatched a group of spies, including their associate pastor, to go one Wednesday and see what was happening at Trinity, to discover why the parking lot was now overflowing across the street. The Grace people had mixed feelings about what they discovered at Trinity. A few were enthusiastic and grateful for God's blessings on their neighbor congregation. A few others were suspicious and jealous, looking for fault and weakness. And a few quietly thought about coming back to Trinity the next week, without the others, because they sensed at Trinity an experience of God's presence and power.

The Gift of God Doesn't Come by Formula

A life-threatening, humbling experience in a pastor's life, a group of women praying, a young person incredibly gifted to lift praise to God with her voice. Each of these events was unplanned. Each was unique to Trinity. The only one of these three things that another church could intentionally replicate would be prayer. But if we look closely at our own lives, we all have our own brokenness. By giving our brokenness to God, we open ourselves to the power of God to renew us, to heal us, and to bless us. No two healing experiences are the same. We have absolutely no control over what God's healing will look like in any particular case. Because healing is God's work, God's grace, it is entirely God's to give as God desires to give it. But in every healing experience, human life is strengthened by God's grace, and we grow in our compassion toward others of God's children in need of similar grace. Similarly, how often God blesses us with people who have the gift of praise, if only we look for them and give them leadership in our worship.

In the third chapter of John, in his famous conversation with Nicodemus, Jesus said these words, "The wind blows where it chooses, and you hear the sound of it, but you do not know where it comes from or where it goes. So it is with everyone who is born of the Spirit" (v. 8). These words unexpectedly came to my mind the first morning I awoke in Nazareth of Galilee, during a visit a few years back. The wild wind would gust a moment, then grow calm, a bit like the Santa Ana winds in Southern California. Jesus goes on to ask his friend Nicodemus how he could be a teacher in Israel and not understand Israel's crazy weather. The point here is the crazy unpredictability and mystery of the wind in Israel. Jesus is teaching that God works in exactly the same manner in our lives.

In the fullness of God's time, God breaks through and touches us today, just as God sent his Son according to an intentional and perfect timetable. We can only wait and hope and trust. On the one hand, we know that soul-stirring music, fervent prayer, bitter disappointments, and failures make us more ready for the visitation of God's presence and power. These things make us ready, but they do not guarantee God's visitation. On the other hand, whenever our music is tamed, our prayer is perfunctory, and our lives are comfortable and successful, the chances are increased that when the wind of God's Spirit blows, we will not notice; and if we do notice, we may turn away.

When the Spirit's winds came to blow at Trinity, people individually decided how they would respond, and many decided to embrace what was happening and take various risks. Several others grew uncomfortable and left. For all the times that the Spirit is glorified in a place, there are also times the Spirit is resisted. For every person in a church who may be ready to embark on a particular journey with God, there will be another who is not yet ready. But when we open the doors and windows of a church to let the wind of God blow through, our faith becomes fresh and firsthand in quality. We remember Jesus anew because we have met him anew, personally and powerfully. And life is never the same again!

I Am the Way

In John's Gospel, Jesus says to us, "I am the way, and the truth, and the life. No one comes to the Father except through me" (14:6). Certainly, the early Christian community's choice to call itself *The Way* is rooted in these words of Jesus. At its first-century roots, the Christian community understood clearly that Jesus was the Way. And the converse of this would be that when we lose touch with Jesus, we lose our Way. It is clear that thousands of Christian communities in our world have lost their Way or are in grave danger of doing so soon if something doesn't change.

When I was a boy, there was a woman in our church who used to sing the song "I'd Rather Have Jesus Than Anything." I suppose she sang other songs too, but this is the only one I remember. It was her song. Her name was Darlene. She and her husband were involved in an automobile accident on an icy Canadian road, an accident that left her unable to walk. I am sure that she and her family must have prayed for the healing of her spinal column. But God's healing, in whatever form it came, never lifted her out of her wheelchair.

As she would sing, "I'd rather have Jesus than silver or gold, I'd rather be His than have riches untold," the same thought always came to my mind: She would rather have Jesus than have the ability to walk again. That impressed me. Darlene knew the Way in life. And every time she sang that song, she pointed us all back to the Way. Knowing Jesus, trusting Jesus, following Jesus, loving Jesus—when a person or a church can do this, they have everything. When they lose touch with this, they have lost everything. If you don't have Jesus, if your church isn't in love with Jesus, if you cannot stand alongside Darlene and belt out those words from the depths of your soul, you will find little help in this book. If Jesus isn't living deep down at the heart of who you are, I invite you to set the book aside and to take some time to pray that God will cause you to fall in love again with the One who died that you might live.

Ultimately, there is no challenge in the life of any person, any church, any family, or any nation that cannot be met if we have Jesus. I hope your church celebrates that and teaches that. And, in the event that you've forgotten this along the way, I pray that God will heal your memory, by whatever means necessary, so that you and your community might bask anew in the same joy that radiated from Darlene's face when she sang that song. Without Jesus, truly we are lost.

Than to be the king of a vast domain
Or be held in sin's dread sway;
I'd rather have Jesus than anything
This world affords today.
　　　　　　　　—Rhea Miller (1922)

Study Questions

1. Is your church more like Grace or more like Trinity, as they were described in the first pages of the chapter? Or is it a blend of both? Explain.

2. Do people at your church feel comfortable talking about their experience with Jesus?

3. How has your experience with higher education challenged your view of the world, your view of miracles and your view of God?

4. How has your experience of trauma or life crisis challenged your view of the world, of miracles, and of God? Have you ever found crisis moments to be points at which you also rediscovered God's reality?

5. Have you ever been a part of a church or a group like the author described from his childhood? If not, do you feel that you are at a disadvantage?

6. Trinity Church's spiritual awakening pushed them from simply thinking about faith to embracing experience. Has any event in your life, your family's life, or your church's life ever pushed you in such a direction?

7. The key factors in Trinity's healing of memory were events that they did not control or cause to happen. Does this mean that God caused these things, or were they simply accidents?

8. Are you comfortable waiting for the Spirit's winds to blow?

9. In your opinion, what exactly had happened to Darlene that gave her such poise and joy?

Notes

1. Blaise Pascal, *Pensées*, rev. ed., trans. A. J. Krailsheimer (London: Penguin Books, 1995), 56.

2. Harvey Cox, *Fire from Heaven: The Rise of Pentecostal Spirituality and the Reshaping of Religion in the Twenty-first Century* (Reading, Mass.: Addison-Wesley Publishing Company, 1995).

CHAPTER 3

REMEMBERING THE HOLY HABITS OF FAITH

Therefore, my dear friends, as you have always obeyed—not only in my presence, but now much more in my absence—continue to work out your salvation with fear and trembling.

Philippians 2:12 NIV

Same Place, Another Time

Cammy and David are president and vice president of the Sunday evening youth fellowship at Bethany Church. One Sunday afternoon, they came to the church a couple of hours early in order to clean out the youth ministry closet.

Bethany is an old congregation, one of the historic churches in this countyseat Maryland town, dating back more than two centuries. Bethany's building, listed on the state register of historic places, bears a cornerstone with the date 1878. Still solid as a rock, both building and congregation, Bethany is a long-standing center of faith and community life for the region. The last decade brought rapid population growth to the county as the Washington, D.C. sprawl crept across Maryland. While many of the historic churches turned up their noses at the newcomers, Bethany seized the opportunity to expand their sanctuary seating and ministry programming, with the result that they entered the new century with record numbers in membership, attendance, and giving. As one of the most affluent churches in the county, Bethany boasted more Rotarians, more physicians, and more attorneys than any other church in town. The Bethany youth ministry, for many decades now, has been known throughout the community as *the* place to be for Christian teens on Sunday nights. In fact, several of the seventy-somethings at Bethany met their mates through participation in Bethany's youth ministry back in the 1940s.

On this particular Sunday afternoon, sixty other middle school and high school students will join Cammy and David. Their motivation in coming early to explore and clean the youth ministry closet was to find cool old stuff for the Bethany youth fellowship float in the town's upcoming bicentennial parade. They found trophies from youth basketball teams in the early 1950s, certificates of honorable mention for the state Bible drill in 1961. They found more than a few rotting Bibles and hymnals, a box of denominational youth Sunday school curriculum from 1974 that someone long ago was supposed to have sent to missionaries in China. They moved slowly through the dust and junk, fascinated by the relics of a world that had passed away.

Toward the back of the closet, David backed into a rusty metal door. Cammy was the first to recognize that it was, in fact, the door to an old safe. As David turned the spindle handle a couple of rotations, Cammy asked, "What song are you singing?" David replied, "I'm not singing. I thought that was you." "No, wait, David, it's coming from inside the safe. It's like there's a radio or something in there." With those words, suddenly the door pulled open in David's hand. As it opened, a smell rolled out that was at once both pleasing and awful, like roses and mustiness. And the music, it sounded as if there were hundreds of people singing together in there, somewhere. The music drew Cammy and David straight through the metal door.

Once inside the safe, they found themselves walking through a hallway. The hallway seemed familiar, yet the walls were covered with pictures that neither of them had ever seen before, pictures of men with beards and women with bonnets. The music grew stronger. "Wait a minute," David muttered as he looked back. "Where we came out a second ago, that's the door to the youth closet." And sure enough, with that point of orientation established, it became clear that they were back in the familiar hallway that ran alongside the sanctuary of Bethany Church. Except, the walls were green rather than white. The floor was wood rather than carpeted. And there were those pictures of strange people with beards and bonnets.

A Church Full of Strangers in Beards and Bonnets

As they passed the side doors into the sanctuary, they paused and listened to the gusty singing:

> And can it be that I should gain
> An interest in the Savior's blood?
> Died He for me, who caused His pain—
> For me, who Him to death pursued?
> Amazing love! How can it be,
> That Thou, my God, shouldst die for me?
> Amazing love! How can it be,
> That Thou, my God, shouldst die for me?

Peeking through the doors, Cammy and David saw the room packed full downstairs, like a Sunday morning crowd. The men wore black suits; the women, simple dignified dresses. A flush of self-consciousness welled up first in Cammy, who, in her summer shorts, seemed woefully underdressed.

"Who are all these people? How did they get into our church?" David thought aloud. "They look like they lived a hundred years ago." And, indeed, across the room was every indication that Cammy and David were not in the twenty-first century anymore. Suddenly, a boy about David's age bolted out of his row and down the side aisle and all the way down to the front of the room. David watched the boy as he proceeded to kneel along the altar rail. One of the bearded men in black came and knelt beside him. It was hard to tell, but it appeared that the boy was crying.

Cammy did not know the hymn they were singing, but she recognized the familiar warmth of the Bethany pipe organ. This was, indeed, her church. She looked over her shoulder, and there, in comforting brilliance, she saw the stained glass window with Jesus holding the lamb, the same as always. But little else seemed to belong here, neither the strange people, nor the old wooden benches. What was going on? She whispered to David, "It's like we're in a time warp or something. This is really weird." David was speechless. Then he suggested, "There's no one in the balcony, let's go up there and watch."

Once in the balcony, they discovered rows of wooden theater chairs, far different from the cushioned seats they and their friends sat on most Sundays. From this vantage point, everything at Bethany looked almost the same, yet altogether different. Then the music stopped and the man in black arose from the altar rail; the boy stood beside him, gazing down. The man spoke: "A sinner has come to repentance, a lost sheep into the Savior's fold. This young man is David Freeman. He comes to confess his faith in Jesus Christ and to receive his glorious salvation."

David Meets David

In the balcony, David and Cammy looked at each other in puzzlement. The young man in the knickerbockers below had exactly the same name as the young man watching from the balcony. Cammy said, "This is too weird. Is that you down there? Why does he have your name?" David then realized and spoke all in the same moment, "He has my name because he is my great-grandfather." And with that, both realized that they had indeed stepped back in time. They said nothing more until the service concluded. The man in black was apparently the minister. As he opened the font and baptized David Freeman, David Freeman IV remembered his own confirmation three years earlier. He remembered the formality of it and how his best friend got the giggles and almost caused the whole row of seventh graders to lose control in laughter. He was struck now by the incredible seriousness of *this* moment, a moment in a year long past, a moment with implications that would trickle down across many years, even influencing David IV's twenty-first-century life.

At the conclusion of the service, David said to Cammy, "I have to go talk to him." Cammy was beginning to worry if they would be able to get back through the door of the safe into their familiar world before youth fellowship began. But she didn't want to leave David in the twilight zone. So the two of them snaked through the crowd to speak with David's fifteen-year-old great-grandfather. When they got to the front of the church, David stepped forward and said, "Hi, my name is David Freeman, too." Met by a look of utter puzzlement, David IV then added, "Look, I need to talk to you, outside, away from these people. Can you meet me outside, in the alley behind the church?" The boy in the knickers nodded yes.

Outside, the world became even stranger than the world within the walls of Bethany Church. Cammy and David were unprepared for the sight of two hundred horses, some with carriages, others tied to trees. Horses everywhere. The hardware store and the bank across the street from the church were gone, now just a field full of horses.

A newspaper blowing in the wind carried the date. It was 1903. As David and Cammy waited in the alleyway, they talked of all the things they could tell his great-grandfather, things about to happen that no one yet knew. The world wars, the space shuttle, the automobile. And then they considered the possibility that

David Sr. would dismiss them both as crazy and believe none of their far-fetched tales.

At that moment, through the shadows, he appeared, just as promised. Introductions were interesting. "Hi, thanks for meeting us. Like I said, I am David Freeman, David Freeman the fourth, and this is Cammy Webster." With that, David Sr. took Cammy's hand and bowed slightly. Cammy's eyes brightened noticeably, despite the twilight. "Where are you from?" asked the young man from 1903. "From here," Cammy blurted, "from Bethany. We all belong to the same church."

David and Cammy proceeded to explain, as best they could, that, technically, they were not even born yet, how they were cleaning out the youth ministry closet when they discovered a door that led from the future to the past. David the older wanted to see this door, so the three of them slipped back into the church building and walked through the hall to the auspicious closet door.

"I want to go through the door," David Sr. said. And before they could respond, he had entered the closet. They followed close behind. On the other side, they found the door to the safe still open and the closet exactly as they had left it. Except, of course, now they could hear the noise of other kids in the building. It was almost time for youth fellowship.

The Strangest Journey of All

As they stepped out of the closet into the hallway, they were met by a group of middle schoolers laughing and running in the hallway. David Sr. was shocked and half-chuckled at the sight of a dozen kids, who looked to him to be dressed in their underwear, running inside his church. "They are running in the church! Why, I've never seen anyone do that before." This would not be the only first for Bethany's twentieth-century guest that night.

David and Cammy decided to take David's great-grandfather to the youth meeting as their guest. Cammy suggested that he take off his bow tie, which he did gladly.

"Oh my gawd," a girl shrieked down the hall, as others giggled. David Sr. was shaken to his boots. He had never heard anyone take God's name in vain in God's house. It was beyond imagination. As the girl ran past him, she called out, "Cool pants!" and disappeared around the corner.

When it was time for the meeting, David Sr. witnessed the rudeness of a group of boys who continued talking to one another even after they had been asked twice to stop. They continued even during the prayer, without any further reprimand from the adults. He looked over at them finally and gave them a big "*shhhhh.*" After the prayer, a band of five teens led into a musical number with a punk sound, which may have been the single most puzzling thing of all for the visiting David. A few sang along, but most just listened or ignored it. David Sr. could not figure out what the point of the noise was. It never occurred to him that this was, in fact, their attempt at worshiping God. He was enamored more with the pulsating images on the wall behind the band, along with the words that appeared out of nowhere on top of the images.

Cammy and David decided to introduce their guest as simply "David's friend David," fearing that any further entanglement of the past and the present might get more complicated than they could bear, perhaps even causing David to be unborn or worse. They couldn't imagine what might happen, but they wanted to be careful nonetheless.

At the end of the evening, David Sr. was more than ready to retreat into his 1903 world, having made almost no connection with what was happening in his home church a century later. The thing that most unsettled him was the sense of casual indifference among the teens that he met, to the point of irreverence in several instances. His last words to David and Cammy before returning through the door of the safe were these:

"Today is a day I will never forget. Thank you for bringing me to see your future world. I feel like I've been to heaven and also to hell in one day. God forgave me of all my sins today and saved me from hell. I was so happy in that moment. And then he allowed me to meet you and to take a journey to see what he saved me

61

from. I will pray for you. Please pray for me. I don't understand the future. I don't understand why the adults of the future let their children come to church dressed like this or why they allow them to act like this. I don't understand why people curse at church or laugh during prayers or act like they have no respect of God. It is all very strange. It scares me if this is what the future is like."

And with that brief extemporaneous commentary, the two Davids shook hands and parted, each to his own time and place.

What on Earth Has Happened to Bethany?

The above tale is not intended as a bashing of contemporary youth culture. Nor does it seek to glorify the past. Indeed, I have watched a couple of generations of youth grow up, both my own generation and the kids I served when I was a youth pastor during my early years out of seminary. In each case, God worked miracles over time, maturing some of the wildest souls into spiritually sensitive and deeply committed disciples. In each case, I saw the powerful traces of God's working while these persons were young, foreshadowing the great things that were to come. I have learned in this way never to underestimate the possibilities of what God can do with a young person's heart. With God, every young life is an unlimited possibility.

The troubling question that we should all be asking is simply whether God is gaining hold of young hearts within our established churches. There are some churches, such as Bethany, at which one would have to reach back a hundred years or more to discover a time when young people were deeply engaged by their church as part of their faith journey. At other churches, it was simply a generation ago. And still in other churches, kids are finding powerful connection with God today, in the context of a local church's ministry.

Bethany Church's theological flavor has changed very little, given the amount of time that has passed. Furthermore, the church reported twice as many professions of faith last year as they did the year David's great-grandfather got saved. Bethany hasn't forgotten who Jesus is. They haven't lost their focus on winning people to faith in Jesus. They stand out in their denomination as a historic church that has remained vital in ministry, though most of their peer congregations have declined both in the numbers of people served and in the coherence of their mission. Yet Bethany is an entirely different place and people than the church that gathered on the same ground a hundred years earlier. Some might conclude the difference is a matter more of style than of substance. But when style becomes as radically casual as it has at Bethany, the substance is affected. Allow me to explain.

The form of Sunday morning worship is *not* casual at Bethany. They still sing many of the same hymns, even to the strains of the same pipe organ (thanks to a million-dollar renovation in 1995). The choir and clergy vestments are more formal than those of a hundred years earlier. So the casualness of Bethany today is not a casualness of form. It goes deeper. It is a casualness of heart.

Casualness of Heart

David Freeman Sr. attended church at Bethany three times a week for most of his life, until he entered a nursing home in 1967. Yet, in that time, he watched the attendance at Sunday evening and midweek services dwindle to a handful, even as the church steadily increased in membership. In the mid-1970s, the Sunday evening service was discontinued, even as the church renewed its commitment to Sunday evening youth ministry fellowship.

David Sr. was raised to believe that personal morning and evening prayer, in addition to family prayer at mealtimes, was basic to the Christian life. Yet, over the years, he began to notice that less was said at church about the necessity of personal piety and devotion. Once during a particularly dry sermon in the 1950s, he briefly entertained the mental question of whether his own pastor spent time alone with God in prayer. He realized that he had never once heard the pastor speak of such. Curiously, he found it impossible mentally to picture his pastor alone with God in prayer. He shook off the thought.

David Sr. was raised to believe that personal repentance and conversion were foundational for membership in a church. Sometime in the late-1940s, Bethany started confirmation classes as a regular annual affair. By the time David's grandchildren came through confirmation classes twenty years later, the main emphasis was on biblical and denominational history. Bethany became a leader in the Christian education movement. But the critical decision cast before the young people at the end of the confirmation course was whether to join the church, not whether to receive the salvation offered through Jesus Christ. Bethany's beliefs about Jesus and salvation had not changed, but the talk was now more about church membership than about repentance.

Perhaps Bethany's greatest change was the increasing affluence of the congregation during the late twentieth century, affording many of its members the opportunity to travel on weekends. Back when David Sr. was growing up, he attended church fifty-one weeks a year, with a week off each July when his family took their annual trek to the seashore. By contrast, his great-grandson, David IV, attended church twenty-five to thirty Sundays a year. The family was still a pillar of the church, but they now owned a million-dollar home on the seashore, a home only an hour away due to the new expressway built in the 1990s. Many weekends were now spent at this second home. In addition, David IV was a crackerjack soccer player, playing in select leagues and tournaments all across the mid-Atlantic region. At least one weekend a month, this involved Sunday games, often three or more hours from home.

Amnesia?

Remember that amnesia is memory loss due to trauma or stress. Would it be accurate to conclude that Bethany's memory loss is stress related? To be sure, Bethany's people have forgotten many of the holy habits that once defined them. Yet, on the surface, one might be hard-pressed to define how the people of Bethany have been traumatized. They have plenty of money and better health care than that of any previous generation. Their local education system and job opportunities are among the best on the planet. They have a higher-than-average percentage of multi-generational families, that is, families with three or more generations represented in the same community. And Bethany Church has been blessed by the cream of the crop in talented pastors for more than a century! So *is* there a traumatic root to the memory loss over the past century? If so, what would it be?

At the turn of the twentieth century, there was no television, no Sunday shopping, no movie theaters, and, for most of Bethany's members, no disposable income after basic needs had been secured. In thousands of communities across North America in 1903, the churches were the center of life.

My own grandparents' lives seemed to revolve around three key activities. They worked hard. They sipped a lot of coffee with family and friends. And they went to church. They went to church at least three times a week, in addition to attending special men's fellowships, women's missionary groups, and youth auxiliaries. When my father was in high school, his junior varsity basketball games were held on Wednesday evenings. My grandparents allowed him to play, but they chose to go to church rather than attend his basketball games. They were making a value statement: that there is a place for youth sports, but spiritual community is profoundly more central to life.

A hundred years later, the typical Christian believers in America place a higher value on recreation, on entertainment, on exotic hobbies, and on travel than did previous generations of believers. In fact, many shrewd congregations today use each of the above activities as evangelistic hooks for the people they are seeking to serve and to teach. In most places, however, these other activities have steadily pushed the amount of time spent in spiritual development downward.

This decline in the amount of time spent in spiritual development activities is, by far, the single most significant change in outward religious behavior among Bethany's members over the last hundred years. If, a hundred years ago, a core member was at church an average of three times a week, for approximately two hours each time and was present fifty weeks out of fifty-two, this yielded three hundred hours spent annually in spiritual development activities with other believers. This is not counting the additional hours building, repairing, and cleaning the church facility. This is not counting time spent in administrative meetings, in personal Bible study, or in preparation for church gatherings. This is not counting all the hours spent caring for the bereaved and the infirm. Three hundred hours a year just in prayer services, Bible classes, and worship.

If today at Bethany, the average core member is at church only once a week (for Sunday morning worship), and attends about thirty-five weeks a year, this yields seventy hours a year in spiritual development gatherings. From three hundred hours to seventy represents a 77 percent drop in the time we spend together intentionally developing our spiritual lives. Of course, accurately surveying an average member's time developing his or her spiritual life is nearly impossible. Estimation is about all we can do here. Your estimate may differ from mine. But all sides should agree that most long-standing congregations have experienced a vast drop in the amount of time people spend gathered with other believers tending to the most important things.

Imagine a 77 percent decrease in our per capita daily caloric intake. People would be suffering from malnutrition and even dying. On a more material level, imagine a 77 percent drop in per capita income. The resulting economic crisis would dwarf even the Great Depression of the 1930s. A 77 percent drop in any critical life resource represents a major trauma.

Might this vast decrease in the time we spend together at church be a factor in our loss of spiritual memory? I suspect so. This loss of meaningful time spent together is especially critical in many congregations' diminishing ability to endow their children with Christian values and habits and to lead them toward a conversion experience.

If We Could Turn Back Time

If we could turn back time, would we? Probably not. Most of us like the present world—warts and all—better than the world of the past. We would choose to keep our health care, our dazzling multi-media connectivity, and all of our technological miracles, thank you very much! What is more important than the fact that we really like the present world more than the past is that there are no gateways in time available to us in the youth ministry closets of our church, where we can escape with those we love to another era.

Or we could, without the convenience of a "magic door," seek to rebuild the world of the past in the present. We could do the Amish thing and dress like the past. We could do the fundamentalist thing and toss out all biblical translations except the King James Version. We could home school our kids (which for other reasons might not be a bad idea). We could join in the grand traditions of many others who, in times past, chose to withdraw from the pressures and stresses of the world in order to create a set of conditions in which their faith could thrive. Both Catholic and Protestant history is filled with various movements that sought to bring spiritual renewal by a measured withdrawal from engagement in the mainstream culture.

Christian isolationism isn't my calling. But I respect it, and I recognize that it may be a valid option for some people. The option of isolation for spiritual communities may be better than business as usual, if business as usual means the slow, steady death of those communities and their spiritual legacy.

Most congregational leaders know that neither turning back time nor isolation are true options for them. But these leaders fantasize that the healing of behavioral memory lies in renewed pursuit of the specific strategies that were effective a century or more ago. According to some of these people, what we need are John Wesley-style Covenant Groups, modeled exactly after the groups who met in eighteenth-century England. According to others, what we need are strong Sunday school classes designed from the brilliant principles employed by the Southern Baptists of the 1940s through the 1970s. For others, what we need to do is bring back Sunday night or midweek worship, during which believers can gather to dig deeper into Scripture and spend more time in corporate prayer than is practical in the *seeker-sensitive/sound byte culture* of Sunday mornings.

There are always a few places where these old strategies will work if we give them a chance. They may, in fact, work almost exactly as they were designed to work originally. Whenever I see these old strategies working well in today's settings, I see the following as well:

1. The senior pastor and the church's core leadership team come to consensus and shared commitment to the strategy. However, when a group of laity seeks to build a renewal movement in their church without the leadership of their senior pastor, the movement is often either marginalized in its effect, or it becomes the source of major congregational division.

2. In the particular community where an old strategy is working, there are certain commonalities with other times and places when a similar strategy worked. Certain communities in rural and Southern America still have living positive memories of Sunday evening worship or strong Sunday school. As long as those positive memories are alive among forty-something adult leaders, our chance of succeeding in the renewal of these old strategies is good. In some communities, the local youth sports associations still avoid Sunday and Wednesday-evening practice times. This helps, too. A few communities still have remarkably homogeneous populations, making the task of gathering folks together in classes and groups much easier than it is in communities with high cultural and political diversity. In more diverse communities, a church usually has to create a strong internal culture of values in order to create the common ground necessary for effectively using the strategies that worked well in a more culturally homogeneous time.

3. Old strategies, though they may flame up and thrive here and there, rarely gain momentum beyond the local setting. There will be a few communities in which enough necessary conditions will be present for old approaches to work, albeit as we contemporize them. But since most communities do not have enough necessary conditions, denominations should be very careful about building future hopes on yesterday's programs and strategies. For every place they still will work, there may be ten places they do not work. And for the places they are ineffective, a church's persistence in trying to make such strategies work may only hasten the church's decline. In other words, the old strategy that still works well in a few places may in fact be causing churches to fail in many other settings.

For each of the above reasons, a simple reconstructing of yesterday is not going to be a valid option in most communities. Most of you reading this book know this already.

This Is Not About the Good Ol' Days

In this chapter, I have chosen to make an important contrast of two different historical moments in a particular church. In so doing, I might inadvertently lead some readers toward trying to reconstruct yesterday, embracing the ways of the past, and "getting back to the good ol' days." Glorifying the good ol' days is not my agenda here. I could have, just as easily, cast this issue of remembering spiritual disciplines by making a contemporary comparison, such as I made in chapter 2 between Trinity and Grace. In this case, I might have chosen to compare Bethany to a sister church in Korea or in West Africa. In many parts of the world today, Christianity is exploding with a brilliance and fire that surpasses even what we saw in the American Great Awakenings that produced Bethany Church of 1903. Setting Bethany alongside these churches of the contemporary Christian frontier, the contrasts would be even more stark. Many of our Korean and African sisters and brothers bring an intensity and discipline to their faith that outshines even the old-timers at

Bethany. Therefore, the amnesia at Bethany should not be dismissed simply as an issue of changing times.

God has not called us to go back in time to minister and to share good news. God calls us to the world of the present, whatever it may look like, whatever values we may discover there, whatever people we may encounter there.

In This Case, Healing Is Going to Take Time!

Whatever strategies God leads us to employ, one of the key elements in healing the lost memory of holy habits is *time*. Not going back in time, but taking some time! We have lost much of the time we once spent together as fellow believers doing the most important things. Increasing the average amount of time that we spend in monthly spiritual formation is absolutely essential. The last twenty years have proved that we can't make New Testament-caliber Christians in one hour a week.

Throughout much of the last century, most old denominations in America measured the strength of congregations with two numbers: total membership and money raised. The Southern Baptists, in the same time frame, tended to measure congregational strength based on two different statistics: average Sunday school attendance and the number of persons baptized each year. I think the Baptists got a better pulse on things with their key measurements than my denomination got with members and money. Nonetheless, all of these old measures are increasingly disconnected with the true strength of congregations.

Over the last few years, I have looked to three numbers as critical measures: average weekend worship attendance, average weekly discipleship group attendance, and the number of persons professing faith in Christ. I have seen too many churches with four-digit membership and seven-digit annual budgets accomplishing perilously little for the kingdom of God.

More recent, in my work as a congregational developer, I have shifted to a new set of four key statistics that offers measures of congregational strength. In these early days of the twenty-first century, I want to know four things about a church in order to assess its health. I want to know (1) the number of people-hours a month in discipleship groups, (2) the number of people-hours a month in ministry, (3) the number of new persons who have made a covenant to be a part of discipleship and ministry groups over the past year, and (4) weekend worship attendance. I continue to monitor total worship attendance to assess balance between the size of the crowd and the number of disciples.

Money and membership are of lesser interest to me in assessing congregational health. Granted, money is a nice thing to have, but poor churches have a more powerful track record than rich churches. Even the annual number of professions of faith tells me very little: In my denomination, if I fall into inactivity just long enough to fall off some church's membership roll, when I join another church, I am added as a profession of faith, with little future commitment expected of me or promised by me.

But if I can measure the total amount of time that people are spending in spiritual formation and the time that people are spending in the exercise of their spiritual gifts (being the church in the world), then I know quite a bit about the relative spiritual depth of a particular congregation. Alongside these measures of depth, I want to be sure that a church is steadily reaching new persons and making disciples of them.

How Often We Become What We Measure

In many old-line denominations, much hullabaloo has been made over a membership decline that stems back to a decrease in birthrates and new member rates in the early twentieth century. As my particular denominational tribe aged, the number of members removed each year continued to increase while the number coming in continued to slip, until, in 1968, we experienced our first net decline in total membership, a decline that continues to this day and shows no signs of changing in our lifetime.

During the 1980s, many folks in my denomination's leadership seemed to awaken all at once to the fact that we were headed toward a dead end if something didn't change. In fact, if the rate of decline were to persist, it was noted that we would cease to exist as a denomination before the end of the twenty-first century. With perfect institutional preservationist predictability, United Methodist bishops across the land began to emphasize and reward pastors for membership growth.

During this period of intense emphasis on membership numbers, two things have happened. First, the membership has continued to decline at an alarming rate despite all of our talk. Second, our anxiety for new members has further cheapened the value of membership. There has never been a time in the history of my tribe when joining most of our churches meant less than it means today. Many of our apparent "flagship" churches have netted membership gains across many years but now maintain a weekend attendance of less than 30 percent of their membership total, and sometimes less than 20 percent. What kind of game is this? In our flurry to grow membership, many churches have become more of a *phone book* than a New Testament church. We can so easily become what we measure.

Lately, many denominations and groups have shifted to tracking average weekend worship attendance rather than church membership as the key indicator of church health. Many of the most studied and most emulated congregations in North America have experienced rapid growth in worship attendance; in many of these churches, worship attendance far surpasses actual membership. Over the last decade, hundreds of historically staid and traditional congregations have added alternative worship services with casual dress, upbeat music, drama, audiovisual enhancements, and greatly simplified liturgy. With the proliferation of these alternative worship services, attendance has spiked upward in many congregations. I have seen few communities in which one could not grow a worship crowd so long as one paid attention to the local culture in terms of music and ambiance and delivered hope and help from Scripture in plain language. At least for the next decade or so, we know how to grow worship attendance in most American communities.

Amazingly, thousands of churches still refuse to use what we know in order to reach out to the people around them. But their continued lack of effectiveness isn't for lack of our knowing how, probably more a result of stubbornness. We know how to build worship crowds. If a congregation or denomination places enough value on this, most are capable of increasing their total worship attendance, at least in the short term.

Yet in many of the churches with the fastest-growing Sunday attendance, less than 10 percent of their adults are involved in any kind of discipleship or mission commitment beyond participation in Sunday worship. My choice to be a part of a worship crowd may simply be a choice to be a religious consumer, to use the worship event as a way of making peace with God, of relaxing on the front end of a new week of stresses and strains.

In our shift from membership to attendance as our core value, we have also shifted from a paradigm of commitment (albeit low commitment) to a paradigm of consumption. In overemphasizing the measure of worship attendance, the church can inadvertently become simply a *crowd*—of strangers.

Just as pastors who have majored in accumulating members have often had difficulty translating membership growth into attendance growth, we are now discovering a new generation of pastors majoring in attendance growth who are having difficulty translating a growing crowd of consumers into a growing core of Christian disciples. I know firsthand from my leadership of a congregation that grew from zero to six hundred in its worship crowd in about two and a half years how difficult it is to take people who enter a community through the worship crowd and to move them toward accountable discipleship. It is often much easier to take people who enter discipleship groups and lead them into large-group worship than it is to take them in the opposite direction.

But What If We Measured Time Rather Than Warm Bodies?

When we choose to measure the number of people-hours spent in various spiritual development activities and in service to God and others, we discover new organizational behaviors and strategies that will increase both the number of participants and the average amount of time they spend with us, growing and giving, especially in small-group settings.

Back in the old days at Bethany, the only regular small-group experience for most people would have been their Sunday school class; and several of these groups were anything but small. Most of the spiritual development time spent at church was decidedly large-group in nature: the worship services, the prayer meetings, the Bible classes, even choir rehearsal. These gatherings varied in size from thirty to three hundred. None of these events pushed people to the level of spiritual intimacy or accountability that is often achieved in a Christian small group today.

More intimacy and accountability is needed today, in great part because it is not 1903 anymore. If people spend six hours a week in large-group spiritual development activity, it will likely have a positive effect on them. But these same people then leave their church gatherings for a world vastly different from the world of 1903. It is a world saturated with almost infinite possibilities for entertainment, both acceptable and unacceptable to Christian sensibilities. Even the acceptable adventures (to the beach house twelve weekends a year or to the weekend soccer tournaments) pose a threat to the primacy of the church as the center of one's life.

Congregations that organize around small groups as their basic building blocks typically have a deeper influence on the lives of participants than do churches that organize around worship crowds as their basic building blocks. In a small-group setting, the following things are almost guaranteed:

1. My presence each week is noticed, as is my absence.

2. I have more opportunity to share personal experience, to ask questions, and to contribute my ideas.

3. My church learns to love and appreciate me for who I am, in my uniqueness.

4. The chances of developing accountable friendships are greater, friendships that enable others to hold my feet to the fire of my stated values and to pray for me daily.

5. If my small group adopts a ministry project, the chance of my active participation in that project is very high.

In fact, churches that are organized around small groups for Christian discipleship and mission often discover that they can accomplish much more in the same six hours a week than Bethany was able to accomplish a century ago. They can accomplish more in terms of the spiritual growth of the participants as well as of persons served in ministry. If we are talking six hours a week as norm rather than two hours, then we have time for *two* other church events each week after we have attended Sunday worship. One of those events might be with peers, sharing, studying, and praying. Another of those events might be more ministry based, using our gifts to be the church in action somewhere in the community. The hands-on experience is often as much a key to spiritual growth as sharing in corporate worship or in small-group discipleship times.

Make such time the key measure of life in a church, and that church will likely be transformed! Measure the number of people-hours in each of the three activities listed above, and it forces us, on the one hand, to push beyond the one-hour crowd and, on the other hand, to strive to add new persons to our community in all three arenas: worship, discipleship and fellowship, and mission. In order to keep the people-hours growing, we are challenged to add both depth (both quantity and quality of time spent together) and breadth (number of persons spending time together) to our ministries.

It Isn't Easy, but So What?

I was visiting with a group of pastors a couple of years ago, and the subject of reproducible small groups came up. A hurried consensus filled the air that the cell-group movement had been proved a dead end: because it was difficult to get people to the groups, because it was difficult to get leader commitments, because it was difficult to get the groups to divide and multiply.

But is "difficult" really a valid excuse for not trying? Imagine a person with a serious disease delaying treatment because it will be difficult. When it's a matter of life and death in our personal lives, we are usually ready to fight and to do and spend whatever it takes to find healing. "Difficult? So what?" When our child is on life support in the emergency room, this is our universal response to the challenge of "difficulty."

Some churches approach their ministry and mission with similar urgency. These churches do what it takes to work around each and any difficulty. They know that an hour or two a week in worship is simply not enough time to do today what we are seeking to do, not enough time for making disciples in a post-Christian and often hostile culture.

I work with church planters in the southeast United States. People from the Pacific Northwest or from eastern Canada may think that church planting in the southeast United States is a picnic. Church planting is *never* a picnic. However, throw in a strong sponsorship commitment by a healthy congregation and a fast-growing middle-class neighborhood, and church planting in the southeast U.S. has a high rate of success.

Take away the strong external funding and the hundreds of new families moving into the neighborhood looking for a church, and the work becomes more challenging. Some of the churches we are planting are not on the growing edge of Bible-belt suburbia. Some are restarts or new starts in the inner city or in communities of population decline. Everything is hard when we plant new churches in such places. Even in suburban communities, where often we see a rush of new church projects from many different groups all at once, the work can become an uphill battle, just trying to carve out a public identity and to find temporary space to meet. Pulling a core group together; defining that group with healthy mission, values, and vision; contending with the price tags of each new step before them—on and on the list of challenges goes for new church planters! It's hard. Each day, a good church planter just nibbles off a bit more, until slowly the job gets done. But most planters go into the work knowing that it will not be easy.

In contrast, many leaders of established churches have not adequately counted the cost of what God is asking them to do. Often they have counted *certain costs* (the cost of seminary, the cost of family disruption, the cost of lots of meetings, visits, and counseling sessions 24/7). But the most important cost each of us should be counting as we go to serve as pastor of an established congregation is this: *What will it take to create a renewed church, a new church, within this old church?* That is what matters most of all! Almost every pastor will ultimately have to plant a church— whether from scratch or within an existing framework—if he or she intends to pastor a vital church. The key is to keep focused on the church we are planting and to resist being distracted by the temptation simply to do maintenance on the existing framework (the committees, the buildings, the worship services, and so on).

Do You Want to Plant a New Church?

Planting a new thing, whether on its own or within the context of a long-existent ministry such as Bethany, is our best approach at raising the amount and the quality of time people spend together each week growing their faith.

A new pastor has a choice: She can major getting into everyone's home the first year and getting to know a lot of folks superficially; *or* she can simply get into a lot of group settings to get face time with an even larger number of persons, with the intent of casting a vision and taking notes on whose eyes light up. Personally, I would choose the "bright eyes" plan every time.

Let's say that I become pastor of a church with 350 members. At the end of the first year, I am up to 360. Yet at the same mile marker, I have gathered thirty visionaries who now have a vision and an experience of church as more than an hour-a-week thing. The headline story of our first year in that place is the thirty visionaries, *not* the net membership gain!

My key task in year two will be to take the thirty to sixty, not to take the 360 to 370. Do you see the radical difference this will

make in the way I spend my time? Do you see the radical difference this will make in the results we will have to show for our
labor by the time we reach the four- and five-year mile markers?
There is no comparison in the level of results we can expect if we
invest our time building the core.

Now, a word of caution. By creating a core, I am not talking
about a group that withdraws to go deep, while the world goes to
hell. I am talking about a core of people who understand that it
takes time together to be God's people. It takes time learning,
sharing, worshiping, and serving. I am talking about people who
are seeking to grow spiritually so that they can exercise the gifts
God has placed in them to minister in the world. I am talking
about people who understand Christianity as *a Way* of life, not
just an affiliation. I am talking about a core group that is a blend
of newcomers to the church alongside persons with significant
history in the church. In almost every case, these core folk will be
involved in a small group, possibly in more than one (settings in
which separate groups form for learning and sharing and for service and mission).

This core of the committed will seldom become the majority
in a church. At times they will simply become the significant
minority who point the church in a different direction.
Occasionally, the committed core will grow to the point that they
outnumber the original church membership many times over.
When this happens, the church may be transformed beyond
recognition. And yet even when the core explodes, there will
almost always be considerably more people attracted to the edge
of the action, attracted to the crowd, attracted simply to come
and watch.

Every turnaround congregation has a story to tell. Every time a
church that had been dying or had been growing older suddenly
begins to grow or become younger, there is a great story to be discovered! Some things are unique about each story. But there are
other things that are the same. Almost without exception, the
story involves the birth and growth of a core of committed
visionaries, the creation of a new church within an old church.
The pastor may or may not have kept a formal roll of the new

church as it emerged, but a new church was being planted nonetheless. A new church sprung up in an old place, sort of like a new lily growing in the springtime from an old bulb.

If you are a pastor and you do not understand your key task to be church planting, you may see only the most modest of fruits for your life's labors.

Back to Bethany

Back to the crazy youth ministry at Bethany, the place we started at the beginning of this chapter. What can be done to help these kids recover a sense of the reverence and seriousness with which their spiritual forebears approached the Christian life? How can their lost memory of the Way be healed?

The answer must address their parents' generation. To focus simply on the youth themselves is to fight an uphill battle in a church where casualness of heart is the norm. To do heart surgery on this church, I would start with adults. I would seek to plant a new church of adults. I would seek to include the youth in the new thing, but not to lead from youth ministry. In order to truly change the culture of Bethany Church we must cultivate a core of committed adults. A few of these new visionaries may be parents of some teens. If so, this is good. If not, that's okay too. The key is that there is a growing group of committed leaders at the heart of Bethany Church who are practicing the holy habits of faith. From this core, the whole tone of life at Bethany will change. The kinds of staff we hire will change. The way we spend money will change. The way we worship will change. And the priorities we set for youth ministry will change.

There may be a youth pastor reading this who will want to protest, saying that I am underestimating the power of a renewal that begins with young people. I would respond by acknowledging that God can start a spiritual revival anywhere he pleases in anyone he pleases. Plenty of spiritual revivals have started with youth. This could happen at Bethany as well. But a youth-based renewal movement may encounter opposition from the church unless it is based in a vision that is shared by the church leadership as a whole. Because of this, youth movements not rooted in adult movements often break away. This isn't necessarily a bad thing: The largest church in America, Willow Creek, was born as an independent youth movement.

But if we are talking about the renewal of *Bethany's* life and memory and *Bethany's* connection to the Christian Way, we need to start at the nerve center of Bethany, with the senior pastor and a core of adults who will lead the way to Bethany's future, affecting every other ministry that is shared under the umbrella of Bethany Church. More about this in chapter 4!

Study Questions

1. Do you see "casualness of heart" in your congregation? If so, what does it look like?

2. How much time do you think the average regular participant at your church spends each week gathered with other believers in spiritual development (worship services included)? Is this down or up from twenty years ago?

3. Do the old strategies of spiritual development (Sunday morning classes, women's circles, youth group, and so on) seem to be reaching and discipling people as well as they once did in your setting? Why or why not?

4. What are the one or two primary measures that your church and its leaders use to benchmark its growth: (a) total church membership, (b) annual budget, (c) average Sunday worship attendance, (d) average Sunday school attendance, (e) annual rate of new members, (f) annual rate of new believers, (g) number of persons involved in the delivery of ministry, (h) the average amount of time regular participants spend in spiritual development and service to others, or (i) other measures (please specify)?

5. Do you think your church should change its focus from the key statistics it monitors? Why or why not? What is the point of monitoring statistics at all?

6. Regardless of whether your church's *crowd* is growing, declining, or flat, what is happening to the visionary core? Does your church have a core of people who "get it," who are passionately committed to Christ and are seeking to express that passion in ministry? If so, is this core increasing in number?

7. How do you feel about the author's belief that adult discipleship is the foundation of lasting congregational renewal and vitality?

CHAPTER 4

REMEMBERING OUR NEIGHBOR

But he wanted to justify himself, so he asked Jesus, "And who is my neighbor?" Luke 10:29 NIV

A Page from Jesus' Playbook

A woman was going from the government housing projects where she lived to the high-dollar part of town where she worked as domestic help. She caught the first bus of the morning, arriving at the neighborhood of her employment before dawn. There, once the bus pulled away, she fell into the hands of an attacker. The man pulled her back from the sidewalk behind the fine public landscaping and raped and beat her, leaving her for dead, her body sprawled upon the ground, partway in public view, under an azalea bush.

As the glow of new morning unfolded upon the bus stop at Bay Boulevard and Champions Green Drive, almost everything appeared like just another day in this, the loveliest part of the city. Flowers were in bloom. A fast food wrapper blew around in the spring breeze. An occasional well-dressed pedestrian zipped along to work. A stray yellow dog sniffed something just off the sidewalk and then trotted on across Champions Green. But there was one thing out of the ordinary this new day. There was a body just off the sidewalk. A woman's legs extended out from under an azalea bush. No blood, just a body.

The first person to step off the bus and actually notice this oddity was a middle-aged woman running late for her morning Bible study group. When she saw the body in the bushes, she stepped away to the far side of the sidewalk and hurried on, thinking how unfortunate that drug addicts and lazy beggars now were encroaching on such a fine neighborhood as this. As she walked away, she strengthened her resolve to vote Republican in the next election.

The next person to notice the body as he came off the bus passed by on the other side. This was a young man, recently converted to the Christian faith. The further he walked away, the more guilt he felt in his heart. Finally, the young man turned around and hurriedly walked back to the bus stop. He reached into his coat pocket for an evangelistic tract, a tiny booklet that posed the question, "If you died tonight, would you go to Heaven?" Carefully, he reached down under the bush and placed the tract in the woman's hand, so that upon awakening, she would read it. Then he hastened upon his way.

Shortly thereafter, another man stepped off the bus, a registered nurse, exhausted from a night in the emergency room of the city hospital, seeking to save broken lives. His eyes immediately spotted the body beneath the azalea bush. He paused and sighed. His mind was beyond numb. Kneeling down, he reached out to check the pulse of the woman. She was alive. Relieved, he stepped back, hoping that she was simply sleeping off drunkenness. As he left, he picked up the curious little booklet that had rolled out of her hand when he touched her wrist. The good nurse walked home engrossed in the reading of an evangelistic tract.

The next two people off the bus were Muslim women, sisters in their midthirties, heads covered, both en route to the hospital to visit their grandmother who had undergone surgery the day before. They saw the body at the same time, and they stopped. Forgetting all about their day's agenda and destinations, they took pity on the lifeless creature underneath the azalea bush. They tried to awaken the woman but discovered that her head had been beaten. One of the women pulled out her cell phone to call for help while the other held the victim's head and continued to speak to her with gentle, loving words. They were seven hours late to see their grandmother that day. The two good Samaritans spent the day at a different hospital, until the injured woman's family arrived. After many days, after much healing had occurred, the woman was discharged from the hospital. She arrived back at her apartment in the projects, only to find two Arab American women in her kitchen, cooking alongside her own sister, the three of them preparing for her homecoming with love.

And the Question . . .

And finally, the question that you probably knew would be coming: Which of these was a neighbor to the woman who fell into the hands of an attacker?

And as you answer that question, the same question Jesus asked in Luke 10:36, stop and pay close attention to the emotions that you are feeling. It is possible that you did not feel quite the same way the last time you heard a sermon about the good Samaritan. You see, the good Samaritan story has been sanitized by too many sweet Sunday school flannel board talks. We don't know any actual Samaritans these days. And so we don't know to be offended by Samaritans. But we do know plenty of persons whose lives do not conform to *our best understandings* of how we ought to live to please God.

You may feel that the above parable was a bit unfair, a cheap shot. You may think of certain people in your Bible study group who would surely stop and help the unconscious woman. You may think of Arab persons, who underwrite suicide bombings, whose lives have been given to the very opposite of love and reconciliation. Yet, even in Jesus' day, there *were* good priests and Levites, even if Jesus did take issue with the corruption of temple worship. And there were *bad* Samaritans, who would have shown no more care for the dying man than the others who passed by.

Or you may feel that the parable sought to suggest that one religion is as good as another. I certainly don't believe that all religions are simply paths to the same end, and so it would be silly for me to press such an agenda here. I would point out that Jesus believed that the Samaritans were on the wrong side of certain issues of belief and practice. Recall that Samaritanism was a heretical sect that had mixed paganism with Judaism. Jesus belonged to a different sect. He was a Pharisee, by his choice. Yet, for some reason, Jesus chose to make a Samaritan the protagonist of his story. Jesus simply saw that our *actions* are, in God's eyes, more profound expressions of what we believe than the mere *words* we recite on the Sabbath. Sometimes, one group has all the right words, but there are *others*, whose faith and lives we may never personally understand, who have the right spirit and who do the right things. Evangelism is sometimes a connecting of our words with their spirit. It is, almost inevitably, a two-way exchange.

It was amazing in Jesus' day, and it is equally amazing in our day, how we can remember all the correct words about God and faith and still step off a bus one morning and act as if we do not get it at all. We are talking about a form of amnesia, the forgetting of our neighbors.

How Did We Forget the People Next Door?

It would seem, perhaps, to be more a case of blindness than memory loss. I mean we interact with diverse neighbors all day long. There may have been a day when we were quarantined by religion or ethnicity into tidy neighborhoods and ethnic zones. But those days are long past. Housing patterns may still reveal a certain segregation, but go to Walmart Supercenter on Westheimer Road in Southwest Houston and you will see as diverse an array of humanity as you will find anywhere on earth. You will discover all manner of lifestyles, all manner of religion and irreligion, all manner of race, all manner of socioeconomic power, all together in the checkout line. Together. The diversity may be slightly less apparent at the large retail store nearest your home, but look closely and you will see it. Or consider the diversity of those with whom you converse and do business online. We live in a global village.

My last book, *Fling Open the Doors: Giving the Church Away to the Community*, explores what it means for a church to rediscover its neighbors and to do ministry with an eye to its neighbors' needs and personalities. One of the central theses of that book is that most churches begin as village churches, churches that reflect the people who live in the immediate area surrounding the church's meeting place. And yet, over time, the church itself becomes an interior community, with its own language and cultural codes. As this happens, the exterior community usually changes. It may grow younger or older, browner or whiter, richer or poorer, more Catholic or more Buddhist. Within only a few years, the church may no longer mirror the surrounding community at all.

The year after I wrote *Fling Open the Doors*, God (with wonderfully divine humor) sent me to a new task and a new office in a very different neighborhood. In my new role as a congregational developer for my denomination, I searched for available office space and found it at an inner-city church. However, the doors at this church are locked at all times. If you hit the buzzer, we look at you through a peephole to decide if we wish to risk letting you in the place. No joke.

The people who belong to this urban church community are a warm and loving bunch, a lot of fun to know. As I have come to know their history, they are actually the remnant of a larger church. Several years ago, about half the original church wanted to relocate to a more suburban part of town. These who remained are the people who said, "This is my church, this is our spot, changing neighborhood or not." I have a lot of respect for that.

However, when I travel up the street in any direction from my office, I see people on the streets and in the yards who look very different from the people I see *inside the gates* of the church. It's two worlds all together! Outside I see brown people, street people, poor working people, and mentally ill people. Inside, I see people much like my own grandparents, looking both ways before they sprint to their cars at dusk without getting mugged. It is an extreme case of community isolation to be sure, but not at all uncommon in our day.

Many attempts have been made across the years by the white grandparents to include the neighbors. But the cultural walls seemed insurmountable, for those both inside the church and on the outside. So both sides gave up, long before I arrived. The world outside seems to have forgotten about this church, except occasionally when they need a few groceries to tide them over until the third of the month, or a voucher to help pay their gas bill. Conversely, the longer I live inside, the easier it is for me to forget about the community, except occasionally when the community hits the buzzer, needing some kind of immediate help.

As I watch the women, the men, and the children who walk past my office to the nearby bus stop, I sometimes wonder if they know the doors are locked. Or if they *care.* I suspect most of the neighbors learned years ago that the church was locked up. I suspect that this is sort of standard knowledge, like the fact that it gets cold in winter or that rich people drive new cars. You can always tell someone who is transient or truly new to the neighborhood when he or she reaches for the locked doorknob before pausing, in puzzlement, to read the signage and hit the buzzer.

The forgetting of neighbor—so glaringly apparent in many of our old central city congregations—is often just as much a reality in suburbia, albeit a bit more subtle. Churches have *gone indoors* in all kinds of community settings, withdrawing from community life except perhaps in a few token ways, such as through cooperation with a local ministry to the indigent or through hyper-focus on abstract social policies and political causes. These kinds of ministries can be valuable. But rarely do they help churches build relationships with neighbors. In many cases, churches now exist simply for two reasons: (1) to hold the hands of their members at the hospital and (2) to provide well-crafted music and words each week that are to the souls of the church members what "comfort food" is to the belly. The neighbor has dropped off the radar.

How did we forget our neighbors? Perhaps the stress of the cultural gaps just wore on us until it was easier to forget our neighbors than to deal with the reality of who they are, how they think, and how they see the world differently from us. It is *the stress of not knowing how* to bridge the gaps effectively, of not knowing how to begin to reach a different ethnic group or a younger generation. Or in those cases in which we knew at least part of what was required to reach the neighbor, our stress may have been rooted more in the *fear* of what changes would be required of us and required of our comfortable churches. Stress-induced memory loss once again. Amnesia, pure and simple.

I work often with churches that have lost touch with their neighbors. Occasionally I will discover people in those churches who harbor feelings of outright hostility toward their church's neighbors, but more often I discover either (a) feelings of frustration about the church's failure to effectively engage and serve the community's people or (b) no feelings at all due to the comforting effects of the amnesia. In the latter case, it is simply "out of sight, out of mind." The neighbors become invisible.

Take a Walk with a Ten-Year-Old

Of course, the neighbors are usually more invisible to adults than to youth and children. To test that theory, all you have to do is take a kid with you on a mission trip, either to the other side of the interstate or the other side of the earth. Take a walk with a ten-year-old down a street in a third-world kind of place, in a place you are likely to pass numerous beggars, many of whom may be women and children. Walk with your child or grandchild down that street. You, the adult, approach the scene with the hardness of your years, with your aversion to welfare, with your knowledge that if you put a quarter in a beggar's hand today, it will be gone by tomorrow. Thoughts of "teaching people to fish versus giving away fish" fill your mind and cloud your vision. And so, groups of American adults walking through such an alleyway will typically band together and say "No denari" to the beggars, one after another, like a continuous loop recording. Or they may just mentally block the beggars out altogether and walk past as if they do not exist.

However, ten-year-olds will typically have no part of such indifference. (I had a ten-year-old a few years back—I know about this.) They want to know why you can't share a little with these persons who appear so desperately in need. Ten-year-olds have little thought of tomorrow or of their inability to alter economic systems. Restraining our impulse to help those who ask for help is a behavior based on abstract principles. Such abstract reasoning makes little sense to ten-year-olds. They just know as they walk this street that they see others in need. The ten-year-old who sees suffering is more likely to feel as if she or he is looking in the mirror, especially if those who suffer are also children with warm smiles, bright eyes, and a common love for soccer. This phenomenon teaches me three things: (1) Most ten-year-olds have not yet mentally closed out the people around them, (2) taking walks with ten-year-olds may be a good spiritual exercise for many of us, and (3) spiritual amnesia has some correlation with age, at least with the onset of adulthood.

This Type of Amnesia Is No Respecter of Theology

Given the emphasis in Jesus' teaching on the value of loving our neighbors, this amnesia is an issue that most Christians would readily recognize as a problem. Regardless of our theological or denominational orientation, most Christian people will confess that they and their churches could do a better job in this arena.

I am not sure that I could say the same about the first two forms of amnesia we have considered earlier in this book. It is easier to find theological mumbo jumbo with which to skate around the issue of who Jesus is. It is easier to skate around the issue of what spiritual disciplines should look like in the lives of healthy believers. But Jesus' teachings are so unambiguous about loving our neighbors, that I have never heard anybody deny the importance of caring for others. Perhaps this is why cooperative ministry ventures (between churches) in local communities most often focus around the issue of serving and caring for neighbors. We all just seem to know and accept that this is a matter at the heart of what it means to be followers of Jesus. As Millard Fuller, the founder of Habitat for Humanity, would remind us, we can all find consensus around the "theology of the hammer."

There was a time, a few decades back, when the categories of "liberal" and "evangelical" did not blur together quite the way they do today. In that era, churches that were more fuzzy about the personal dimensions of faith and about the importance of orthodox beliefs were often more passionate about the ministry of loving neighbors. In the 1960s, churches that were more emphatic about converting the lost and nurturing a personal relationship with God were often remarkably unconcerned about the worldly needs of people. Today, this polarity is rapidly disappearing. In fact, evangelicals sometimes have more energy for social ministry than their more liberal sisters and brothers. Everybody today loves to build Habitat houses, it would seem. And nearly everybody will admit, when we gently press the issue, that they wish their churches were doing more tangibly to express love for neighbors.

In long-established communities, in which folk have known one another across many years and multiple generations, often the never-ending drama of interpersonal relationships steals our attention from our neighbors. In such cases, members of the church become focused on watercooler conversations that reveal tidbits from the latest episodes in people's lives. During the writing of this book, I found myself in such a church one Sunday. This church had a great location, great facilities, great music, a talented pastor, and yet many of the people had known one another all of their lives. They knew before they got to church (1) whom they would talk to, (2) where they would sit, (3) whom they would lunch with, and so forth. In such a church, so busy socializing with itself, it is difficult to give proper attention to newcomers and harder still to focus on the people who have never even darkened the doors of the church. This church, doing so much of its ministry so excellently, was puzzled why they were declining and why so many of their visitors never returned. So far as I could tell, this particular case of amnesia was not trauma based. It appeared to be simply a result of a distracting concern with their social lives and family relationships within the church community.

What About Social Justice?

Many churches today have translated Jesus' call for loving neighbors into a passion for seeking to change laws and public policies so that the poor and dispossessed have a better shot at educational opportunities, living wages, health care, and the like. Sometimes these churches make a constructive contribution toward the building of a more just society. In thousands of congregations across America, "social justice" is the beginning and end of the church's mission. However, most social justice congregations stop short of actually sharing their faith in Jesus Christ with their neighbors in a way that invites the neighbors to join them in discipleship. In fact, though exceptions do exist, most social justice congregations receive only a trickle of new members of any kind. These churches may cook down to tiny bands of believers, rattling around in large sanctuaries like ghosts of the congregations who once worshiped there. They are drawn together as much by their political instincts and urban lifestyles as by their faith in Christ.

For every church in which the passion for social justice is truly embraced by the grassroots membership, there are many others in which the pastor alone (or the pastor and a small inner circle) crusades for a certain vision of social justice, while the rank and file yawn. They yawn because they live in another world from the dispossessed, and they bring to church an entirely different set of life concerns. Their minister's passionate crusading scores a giant disconnect. These church members are suffering from the very amnesia that we are considering in this chapter. But the crusading pastor may also be suffering from the same amnesia, if his or her focus is simply on abstract public policy. Bottom line, if we aren't actively fostering real-time relationships with the neighbors we are seeking to help, we are probably missing the boat.

Clearly, there *is* a place for public policy concerns in the life of Christian churches! No doubt God calls certain congregations to be political, to be determined in helping to effect certain realities in public life. But commitment to public policy change does not in itself represent an adequate response to Christ's calling to be in community with our neighbors. Public policy concerns, where they arise, should come as a by-product of our first getting to know our neighbors. Creating relationship must be the first priority. It is in relationship that we truly discover our neighbor. It is in relationship that we are changed by our neighbor. And it is almost always in the context of relationship with believers that neighbors decide to become followers of Jesus. Christian love is, first of all, about breaking bread together where we can see the whites of one another's eyes. Christian love is about knowing people's names and praying for people *by name*. Christian love is about hearing people's individual stories and offering a custom response. Building systems that effectively deliver help to meet people's needs on a large scale—this is important. But even more important than generic systems-based responses is our stopping to treat people like precious children of God, unique in all of creation. Love is personal. Out of personal experiences, we are motivated to create just social systems.

Recently, my denomination's central leadership extended a call to the churches to take seriously Christ's call to minister to the millions of American children who live in poverty conditions. I was privileged to sit through two speeches relating to this challenge, one by a political lobbyist from my state's capital and another by one of our bishops. In both cases, their call was for us to get educated about poverty statistics and lobby our representatives for measures that would alleviate the poverty. In both settings, I looked around me and watched the people in the audience fidgeting, looking at wristwatches, and occasionally even rolling eyes. In neither case was any call extended to the church to go out and actually do ministry with poor children in our midst, a call that would have been much more readily received. The most obvious starting place in our learning to love poor children was thus ignored. And since most of the people who heard those two speeches did not know any poor children personally, there was a huge disconnect.

But what if we challenged the people of God to serve poor children and their families, to create ministries in which we get to know real people with real names, real personalities, and real life challenges? If I could get the fifteen hundred people who attended the bishop's speech actually to get to know some poor folk, then their political perspectives would be appropriately challenged and much more effective lobbying would occur, naturally.

The point here is that it takes relationship with our neighbors to cure our amnesia. In order to remember our neighbors, we first have to meet the neighbors.

Meet the Neighbors

I know one church that recently celebrated an anniversary. However, rather than bringing back a former pastor and looking inward and backward, this church celebrated with a block party. They used their anniversary as an opportunity to meet the neighbors. They went door-to-door through the community, inviting the neighbors to an outdoor barbeque. A few weeks later, they followed this up with another outdoor festival, designed with the church's neighbors in mind. In these two events, they met scores of new neighbors with whom they had never interacted.

I know this church because I used to serve as the pastor there. I had nothing to do with either of the above events, but I am happy this church continues to see itself more as a community center than a temple. A church with a self-understanding of its physical facility as a community center will have a much easier time meeting the neighbors than a church that understands its building to be a temple in which the insiders gather, apart from the world.

I recently spent a remarkable weekend with the Cornerstone Community Christian Church in the northern suburbs of Toronto, Ontario. This seven-year-old predominantly Chinese Canadian congregation has collected pledges toward the construction of their first building—a community center that will serve as a hub of multicultural life and a bridge to help them build relationships with their neighbors of *all* races. More encouraging than the large amount of money this young church pledged for land and building is that they also pledged to build relational bridges right now, long before any dirt is moved or bricks are laid for a facility.

As I expressed in *Fling Open the Doors*, every congregation needs a community beyond itself in order truly to be a church. Congregations that lose this sense of their larger *parish* responsibility will inevitably decline. Such congregations may be situated in contexts of growing population where transfer growth from other churches can swell their membership and attendance for years to come. And yet, without a sense of purpose and mission beyond themselves, such churches often greatly undershoot their growth potential and begin declining even while community population is still growing. Among those who unite with such churches, the percentage of members that remains involved in church life and worship on a weekly basis often runs below 25 percent. A church without a mission beyond itself bores most people eventually, even most of its own members.

A church may be largely estranged from the people who dwell in the neighborhoods around its facility and still be a church that is open to particular groups of people from beyond its own membership. Such a church may be effectively engaged in ministry with and to those people. For example, a historically African American church in a community that is now mostly Spanish-speaking, may still be a vital black church if its target community is still finding its way in and out their doors. Ethnicity, cultural heritage, specialized ministries, and other aspects that give a sense of unique personality to a church—all of these factors can help create a connection between a church and a *virtual neighborhood* that may extend all across a region.

I still feel sad whenever I see a church that is utterly oblivious to the people who live around its facility, even if that church is effectively reaching and serving certain population groups across a wider area. Nonetheless, the major issue for every church, finally, is to find a community beyond itself, *any community*, to find some neighbors, *any neighbors!* Find people groups and individual people within those groups. Find people from beyond your church to whom you feel a special calling to love. And then love them! Love them one by one. Learn them by name.

One of the reasons I enjoy working with mission developers who are planting new churches is that these folk start with few, if any, insiders. They have to deal with the community. They have to discover the neighbors. Withdrawing into pastoral care of those already gathered is simply not a viable option for a mission developer. Neither is it an option to withdraw into administrative concerns. A new church start will fail unless the leaders spend time meeting the neighbors and discovering a sense of affinity with the people in the place they are seeking to plant the church. Is it any wonder, then, that groups and denominations that emphasize new church development typically reach two to ten times as many nonchurch people in such projects as they will reach through even their most outreach-oriented congregations.

During the first two decades of this new century, we are going to witness a new phenomenon on the part of a few central city churches in which the members are mostly commuters from other parts of town. We might call this new phenomenon *re-neighboring*. In re-neighboring, a group of families in a central city church decide to sell their suburban dwellings and move en masse to a neighborhood near their church's facility. The fundamental motivation for these folk is not "This Old House" stuff, though reno-vating an old house can be part of the fun. The point for these missioners is the opportunity to integrate themselves into the life of an economically and socially stressed community, so that their church might be in mission to its neighborhood up close and not from a distance. These are people who have recognized that it is almost impossible to meet and serve neighbors from a distance. They see that the best hope for their church's neighborhood is not simply throwing federal or church funds at the challenges, but, rather, throwing themselves *in relationship* to the neighbor-hood. Some beautiful stories will be written around this theme in the years ahead.

Three Universal Keys to Drawing Out the Neighbors

As far as I can tell, there are at least three keys to our neigh-bors' hearts that are valid in nearly every community setting and on every continent. These keys are (1) indigenous music, (2) lov-ing our neighbors' children, and (3) good food. No matter where a church is doing ministry, most people love music, children, and eating. Any church that is ministering effectively on all three of these fronts is probably thriving.

Indigenous Music

Almost every culture is crazy about music. However, only a handful of people in most communities are crazy about the music we typically sing at church. If the music a church is singing has not changed significantly in the last decade, chances are that an insider musical culture has emerged in the church that the neighbors will not appreciate. It seems so painfully obvious (this isn't rocket science), but we need to be singing stuff that the neighbors will enjoy singing with us. When our music comes to be dominated by our denominational hymnal, accompanied by the same instrumentation that would have been used in 1970, sung to the same tempo, we have taken the greatest draw God has given us for reaching our neighbors and squandered it.

Listen to the music that the neighbors love, and sing music that emerges from what you learn as you listen! Enlist musicians who know how to make such music. You will find the musicians you need more often in the neighborhood rather than in the church membership. In all likelihood, if we all listened to the music our neighbors love, then very quickly drums would replace organs as the common denominator in church instruments across North America. Good pipe organs will be around a long time, and they will bless multiple generations to come. But pipe organs are often million-dollar items. Electronic organs are affordable, but they make a whiny sound that many people today find offensive. The church organ will not be the instrumental key to reaching the masses that God is calling us to reach in this century. Pipe organs may help us rally a few intellectuals and high-culture types in Minneapolis and a few died-in-the-wool multigeneration Presbyterians in Dallas. A pipe organ will certainly help reach Paul Nixon, if the church's mission focus is reaching umpteenth-generation Christians like me who have attended church non-stop since they were two weeks old. I *love* pipe organs. But that fact is largely irrelevant to me, since God calls me not to reach myself, but to reach my neighbors!

Now, if we would simply invite some new musicians onto the organ bench, the church organ could, in certain cases, be salvaged for mission as part of a high-energy instrumental ensemble that makes some really *winsome* music (to the neighbor's ears). This may be truer in the African American community; but music is an ever-changing phenomenon. I use the term *winsome* because anything we are doing that does not help us *win some* people to be disciples of Jesus is something that we need seriously to reevaluate. I will make a shot in the dark and predict that 80 percent of the growing worship communities in North America in 2010 will have *extremely innovative* music that is in sync with the musical sensibilities of the neighbors who are choosing to attend those services. Most of the 80 percent will not use an organ at all. Thus, any church that refuses to sing in new musical languages is choosing a ministry strategy that offers an 80 percent guarantee that it will either die or become marginalized in the community. Worship wars notwithstanding, these are the stakes in the choices we make about music.

Loving Our Neighbors' Children

In most communities, children are the easiest group to reach. They have an amazing openness that Jesus observed many centuries ago. They tend to have time on their hands. And, in many cases, they have not yet been taught by experience that church is a boring, irrelevant place. So we usually have a shot at getting to know our neighbors' children, even before we may be able to get to know our neighbors.

So long as a church cultivates its reputation on the community grapevine as a trustworthy, safe, and fun place for children, many unchurched adults will readily allow the church to partner with them in raising their kids. Parents are almost paralyzed by the fear of drugs and other demons that threaten to destroy their children. Providing a safe place after school during the latchkey hours; providing tutoring; teaching music, art, or other disciplines that have been cut from public school funding; providing organized recreation: these are services that parents are often willing to receive from the church for the benefit of their children.

Insofar as the ministries that we provide to community children offer regular opportunities for the parents to come and see their children *perform* (whether it be on the basketball court or on choral risers), we are afforded an opportunity to meet the parents and to get to know them as well. Those times when community parents come onto a church's site to see their kids perform are moments when the need for hospitality exceeds Easter Sunday morning! I cannot overstate this point. The more we create a welcoming and culturally indigenous environment for the parents (so that their language, their clothing, their sense of humor, and other tastes are affirmed), the better chance we will have of seeing those parents again in the future, both at children's events and other settings.

Again, as I stated at the end of the last chapter, youth do not build churches; adults do. Youth are not the future of local churches; adults are. Children and youth usually move away to a new part of town or a new part of the world by the time they are raising their own children. Thus, in a mobile society, they rarely will grow up to become the long-term building blocks upon which a particular congregation is built. Jesus' disciples were adults; a few were young adults, but they were adults nonetheless, not children. *Healthy congregations are built upon a foundation of solid, constantly expanding, adult discipleship systems.*

Nonetheless, I believe passionately in youth and children's ministries for two main reasons:

> 1. *Jesus loved kids and saw the value of investing time and love with them.* We plant the seeds of a tree whose shade we may never see when we lead children to Christ. That's a good thing. Furthermore, Jesus saw how interaction with children is vital to the spiritual formation of adults.
>
> 2. *Youth and children's ministries, done right, draw adults into our orbit, adults whom we must win and disciple.* Let's go get the kids, but let us do so with the end goal in mind that we are seeking to grow the church's core by making disciples of adults.

Good Food

In the fall of 2001, a handful of people in the church where I was pastor came up with a novel idea. They proposed that our church throw a big Thanksgiving dinner for the community. The team sponsoring the dinner would prepare the turkey and dressing. They would do so with profits accrued from the church's weekly community café. The meal would be at noon on Thanksgiving Day, meaning that the vast majority of the church membership and the larger population would be unable to attend due to prior family commitments. But this dinner was not for the church membership; though some members did attend. If it had been for the membership, we could have held it on the Sunday before Thanksgiving. Similarly, the meal was not simply for the poor; though we issued invitations to families in economic crisis through our local food bank for several days in advance. This meal was for anybody who needed a big family for Thanksgiving. It was for people whose family members were not "coming home," for other people who lacked resources to purchase a feast, for others who lacked the energy to cook one, for still others who desired to "rent a family" for three hours, for a few who were estranged from their families. We turned on big-screen football. We told people to bring food if they wished. Some did, others did not. The loaves and fishes thing happened with the food. We could have all survived for a week in there. Two hundred people showed up, and we shared in the most meaningful and memorable Thanksgiving dinner I have ever known. It was a cross section of the community. Those who brought food typically chose the very best recipes in their arsenal.

It was every bit as culturally eclectic as the first Thanksgiving. We broke bread together as strangers and neighbors, and we became friends. It is amazing how much ground can be gained in terms of relationship when we simply sit across from one another at a table and share a meal together. Table fellowship is a powerful thing.

In Acts 2:42-47, we have the famous description of the Jerusalem church in the first months of its existence. Here we discover a list of the things that these believers did in their life together. In this litany of activities, *there is one thing that was listed twice*. Among the varied activities of this primal church, they gathered for Sunday school (seven days a week), they shared laughter and tears and prayer requests, they pooled their material resources, they helped *anyone* who had a need, they worshiped the Lord, and they chowed down. But only the last activity on the list comes up twice. In verses 42 and 46, we are told that they "broke bread" together. As vital as prayer and teaching are to the Christian movement at its headwaters, as vital as missional outreach is, these things are mentioned only once. The only activity that is mentioned twice is that they loved to eat together.

This teaches me that a church simply cannot do its mission without an intentional regular effort to bring neighbors together to share a table and eat. If your church has a soup kitchen ministry, I hope the church members are not all hiding behind the serving table or back in the kitchen. I hope you *all* sit down with the folks you serve and break bread *with* them. If your church has a midweek dinner, I hope that you would consider offering it to the community, without the inconvenience of requiring reservations. Few restaurants in your area require reservations, and, amazingly, few run out of food. They even manage to make a profit and to pay the rent, something not required of a church-sponsored café. The restaurants in your community have proved that reservations are not necessary, except to kill business. If your church cannot figure out how to offer food without reservations, I would encourage you to ask one or two of your area's restaurant owners to teach you how they do it.

The Pot of Gold at the Foot of the Rainbow

Once we have, by God's grace, remembered how to be neighbors again, then the best begins. This is true with the healing of every form of spiritual amnesia addressed in this book: As we are healed, God has surprises for us, blessings that we would never have imagined in advance but that are means of grace to us, helping us never again to forget the most important things.

In the summer of 2002, Rob Gulledge was appointed as pastor to the old Government Street United Methodist Church in historic downtown Mobile, Alabama. This church and its imposing Spanish Colonial cathedral sanctuary have been a fixture in Mobile for over a century. The church was about to close, with only a dozen active members remaining, half of whom were in their nineties. A massive, old building was literally crumbling around them. Then, one of the few remaining members died, and she surprised the church with a $250,000 bequest. The bishop consented to leave the church open if they would use the bequest to invest in new leadership and ministry. The mission developer-pastor's salary was to be paid from the bequest for the first two years. The bishop said, in love but with all seriousness, "Anything your new pastor asks you to do, do it."

During Rob's first summer, he began collecting new friends in the city. As he did so, attendance began to creep up into the thirties, into the forties, into the fifties. Fifteen weeks into this turnaround project, the church made an all-out effort to invite the community and many of the downtown workers to a September 11 memorial service. Two hundred and twenty people came along with the local TV cameras, and Government Street Church was on the score-board at the bottom of the first inning of a new ballgame.

On the weekend before this important community event, several people at the church decided to have a cleaning day, pulling weeds, planting flowers, and so on, like a family "getting ready for company." As they attacked the overgrowth between the side-walk and the sanctuary's east wall, they discovered that they were uncovering a man's home, the dwelling place of a street person who lived in the bushes. They met a new neighbor in those bushes, a man named Keith. And out of respect for him, they left the bushes a bit high in that spot to preserve his privacy.

Keith, the new neighbor, was not really a brand new neighbor. He had been living literally up against the wall of the church building for more than a year, sleeping in the bushes, and grilling on his little hibachi. And yet no one at the church had ever seen him before. Equally remarkable was the fact that Keith thought the church had been closed for most of that year, expressing grat-itude now that it had been opened again. In reality, never a Sunday had passed during the year of Keith's residency in the shrubs that the sanctuary of Government Street Church was not opened so two or more could gather and the old pipe organ could wail. How odd that a person who lived with his pillow pressed against the outside walls was totally unaware of this, week after week! As they would say in the medical business, there was no detectable pulse at Government Street Church.

As of this writing, Keith hasn't come inside for worship services yet. But he is fast becoming a friend of Government Street Church, functioning as the self-appointed night watchman who walks the property each evening to see that all is well. In a matter of days, Keith went from invisible stranger to unpaid staff member. Because Keith is on the radar of Rob and company at Government Street, all kinds of good things are in store for him. Through the deepening of relationship, Keith will share more and more of his story and those who listen will share more and more of theirs.

But the pot of gold at the foot of the rainbow is the gift that Keith brings to the church. Suddenly, this place where he lives is more than simply his house. He is aware that it is also God's house, and he wants to protect it at night, to offer his gifts in service. I wonder, in seasons past, how many hundreds of derrieres, attached to the bodies of persons who did absolutely nothing in ministry, have warmed pew cushions in that sanctuary. Yet here is a person who probably doesn't even feel worthy to sit on a red velvet cushion, who is joining the Government Street ministry team at the bottom of the first inning of a bright new season. Multiply Keith times the hundreds of other neighbors who have gifts to offer God and to the community, and you may begin to get the picture. Our neighbors are treasures to be discovered, to be loved, to be enjoyed, and to be celebrated!

Once we are in meaningful relationships with some of the diverse people who live in our neighborhoods, it is amazing not only how much more effective our ministries will be, but also how much more fun life becomes and how different life will look like to us as we step off the bus on the corner of Bay Boulevard and Champions Green Drive.

Study Questions

1. What particular thoughts or emotions came to you as you read the parable of the good Samaritans at the front of this chapter?

2. Was your congregation ever more of a "village church" than it is today? In other words, did it once more fully reflect the people who lived around its building than it does today? What would it take for your church to become more of a village church once again?

3. Is conversation—even this conversation—about the people we are failing to reach causing the stress to rise in you and in the others around you? Why does this happen? How do we cope with such stress?

4. What reason did the author give for some churches growing in membership, but dropping in weekly participation to 25 percent (of membership) or less? Has your church ever experienced this phenomenon? What might you do in response?

5. What are the three keys to the neighbor's heart? Which of these three seems to offer a place from which your church could step out in ministry to your community?

6. What did Keith, the homeless man, teach Government Street Church? What might he teach your church?

CHAPTER 5

REMEMBERING HOW TO BE EFFECTIVE

I have become all things to all people, that I might by all means save some. 1 Corinthians 9:22

The Story of Big Creek

Once upon a time, long before the post–World War II housing developments to the north of a certain Southern American city, there was a small farming community called Big Creek. Big Creek had two churches, a Baptist church and a Methodist church—Calvary Baptist and New Harmony Methodist. The combined membership of the Baptists and Methodists was composed of all but six of the fifty-seven families in the little community. Calvary Baptist had always been the larger of the two churches, but not to the point of dominating the community. In 1950, Big Creek people split roughly 60-40 between the

Baptists and the Methodists, respectively. More than once, when Calvary was between pastors, they invited the pastor of New Harmony to serve as their "pulpit supply" pastor for a few months until they could find a good Baptist "preacher boy" (Calvary took pride in calling and training young pastors). Each summer the two churches would join together for revival services. Though these services were usually held at the Baptist church, whose building was larger, they would swap back and forth between a Baptist evangelist and a Methodist evangelist. On the even years, when the preacher was Baptist, they would seek a music leader who was Methodist, and vice versa. Many of the people in the Big Creek community could cite particular experiences of personal spiritual awakening in one of the summer revival meetings. The annual summer revival service thus made good sense as a method for the spiritual development of Big Creek people in those days.

Because of the interchange between the two congregations, the only substantive differences between the two were that the Methodists would baptize your baby if you liked and they had a brick church house, while the Baptists had only wood siding.

Sometime in the mid-1960s, the Baptists called a new pastor who no longer wished to share in the joint summer revival. Thus it was that the Baptists and Methodists began holding *separate* revival meetings in Big Creek. About this time, Calvary Baptist built a brick building, considerably larger than the Methodists' building. And Calvary bought a fleet of used school buses and launched a bus ministry to transport children to their church from the new subdivisions dotting the landscape between Big Creek and the growing city to the south. Calvary also began creating new Sunday school classes and emphasizing small-group connections among people. This was the same era in which New Harmony's Sunday school participation fell behind its worship attendance. During the period from 1964 to 1972, Calvary created thirty-two new classes. New Harmony created none.

In the early seventies, Calvary's choirs exploded in size as the church invested in a full-time minister of music. Soon their senior high choir began touring all over North America in the summer. Even some of the Methodist youth joined the Calvary

Baptist youth choir. With the power of high energy and high-quality music in their services, Calvary's people began to approach each Sunday with a level of anticipation and expectancy akin to kids on Christmas Eve. With such high energy now marking Calvary's worship on a sustained basis, the Baptist church discontinued their annual revival services. They did not feel they needed them anymore. Meanwhile, the Methodists grew older, and the old folks looked forward each summer to the revival, where they could sing the old songs, several of which the Baptists still sang all during the year.

In 1980, the Baptists changed pastors for the second time in two decades, and the new pastor came in with the vision that Calvary should begin broadcasting their worship services on television. Beginning on a small UHF station and switching within a few years to what would become a nationwide cable network, Calvary began sharing good news with thousands of people across their region, people who had never before walked through their doors. Over the course of the 1980s, Calvary's music evolved to a blend of high-quality country gospel and Christian contemporary, along with a continued smattering of deeply loved classics.

Meanwhile, New Harmony was experiencing anything but harmony at this point. In fact, New Harmony Church split in 1985, after a lengthy brouhaha over which hymnal they would use. The group that favored returning to the 1939 hymnal prevailed. As Calvary was marching boldly into a new century, New Harmony was marching back toward 1939.

By the mid-1990s, the population of Big Creek had grown from a few hundred to about forty thousand people. Despite the split, New Harmony was proud of the fact that they had retained about the same number that they had forty years earlier—eighty-five or so on a typical Sunday. During a period in which their denomination had actually lost membership, they had actually netted a 20 percent gain on roll. In the same forty-year time frame, Calvary had grown from 150 on Sunday to about 3,000. By the late 1990s, the median age at Calvary was thirty-five. The median age at New Harmony was sixty-eight. New Harmony voted in 1998 to refurbish their historic sanctuary at a cost of $100,000. That same year, Calvary built a 4,000-seat worship arena in which the multimedia and sound systems alone cost over $400,000. In the year 2000, Calvary launched an interactive website that allowed people around the world to order sermon tapes and make their offerings online. That same year, New Harmony voted, after a ninety-minute business session, to buy a desktop computer for the church office so their part-time secretary could assist their volunteer treasurer in the posting of contributions.

The two churches were now separated by a freeway and a large regional mall. Big Creek had been annexed by the city and no longer thought of itself as a separate community. In fact, few people at either church remembered the days when they were just two country churches serving a small community, arm in arm.

Over the previous years, both churches had experienced controversy and conflict between members' points of view. These conflicts nearly paralyzed New Harmony at a couple of points. At Calvary Baptist, however, the majority of Sunday worshipers never knew about their youth minister's extramarital affair in the midseventies or the controversy over redefining the role of deacons in the early 1990s. In short, Calvary had such momentum that the typical conflicts and controversies of church life were more easily absorbed and forgotten.

The story of Calvary and New Harmony in the latter half of the twentieth century is a story of how two churches, both thriving in 1950, responded differently to massive changes in their community and in the tastes of popular culture. As a result of their responses, one church was able to change and embrace thousands of people. The other turned inward, looked backward, and fell so far behind the curve of social change that no one was able to imagine how they would ever be able to reconnect with the community around them. New Harmony Church gradually forgot how to be effective in ministry. In an era in which the various technologies of effectiveness were advancing at a dizzying pace in many disciplines, New Harmony lost touch with the movement of technologies relevant to their mission: the technologies of transportation, communication, and music, just to name three.

How Do We Forget Technology?

Technology is, of course, an ever-changing enterprise. So it may seem odd to speak of the church forgetting technology, when it may appear to us that the church never learned it to begin with. For example, we may be part of a church that, like New Harmony, lags behind in the communication revolution. We may still be a church of overhead projectors and hymnbooks in an age of PowerPoint. Yet our church may once have been cutting edge in terms of communication and effective means of ministry. It is not that we forgot how to do PowerPoint. We never knew anything about PowerPoint. We may just now be getting comfortable using WordPerfect rather than the old IBM typewriter. The point is not that we forgot any *particular* technology, but rather that we forgot *how to be cutting edge in the various crafts of ministry.* And any church that has forgotten how to be cutting edge has also likely forgotten *what it feels like* to be cutting edge.

I have served as a pastor in both kinds of churches. I have been to Calvary, and I have been to New Harmony. I think I understand something about both places.

As for being a leader in a church on the cutting edge of ministry technology and strategy, all I can say is that it's a lot of fun! Being a part of a church that is daring to step out and embrace the future and to embrace people in creative and newly emerging ways feels a lot like being part of a winning team. More often than not, highly innovative churches also happen to be experiencing Pentecost all over again: people coming to faith in Christ, increased "goose bump" kinds of moments in worship, and energy toward deepened spiritual commitment among the core of leaders and participants.

I've also spent some time at New Harmony. All I can say about that is that it's more fun over at Calvary!

New Harmony, New Harmony, New Harmony. Where shall we begin? Let's begin with the sick feeling I used to get when the Calvary newsletter came in the mail—not literally the *Calvary* newsletter, of course, but the ever-expanding good news from the thriving churches either in my own community or in my denominational tribe. By my estimate, there will be a lot more New Harmony pastors than Calvary pastors reading this page (the New Harmonys in the world outnumber the Calvarys by ten to one, at least), so I am sure that I am not alone here in my experience of the sick feeling when the latest round of good news breaks from the giant party going on at the church down the road.

The absolutely enormous offerings and overflow crowds at Calvary can be quite intimidating to those of us back at New Harmony. Where do all those people come from? How on earth are they motivated to give all they give and to do all they do? Of course, those folks are caught up in the rush of being a part of God's winning team. Back at New Harmony, the only rush anyone can remember is the rush to get out of Sunday worship service before the cars start pouring out of the Calvary lot, so they can find a lunch table without having to wait in line.

At New Harmony, there are several counterproductive ways we may cope with the natural stress of inferiority as we see churches flourishing around us. Here are three:

- We may choose *to demonize the Calvarys in the world,* to look for their faults and excesses, to comfort ourselves with the belief that Calvary is, for all practical purposes, cheating. Often, this *cheating myth* is accompanied by the belief that we, the struggling ones, are like the faithful remnant in Isaiah. I will say more about this in a moment.
- We may choose *to give up the dream of making a difference in the world and to turn inward.* With this strategy, we cease paying any attention to Calvary and also cease watching the changing tastes of the community around us. We simply seek to care for one another and

take comfort in the familiar. The world is changing
too fast anyway.
• We choose *to turn our energy and anxiety on one
another* at New Harmony. It is amazing how, as
churches slip out of the game, the members begin to
steer the energy that they should be putting into
vision and ministry toward internal conflict. Very
often, churches like New Harmony are deeply con-
flicted churches, controlled by two or three families.
The conflict and control may be a long tradition in
the congregation, in which case we know why the
church chose to withdraw and decline rather than to
change and expand in the first place. However, conflict and control often seem to arise and to snowball
after the church stagnates.

In each of the above ways, the end result is the same: We isolate ourselves further from behaviors that would help us reach
others in the community. Insofar as we isolate ourselves from
churches like Calvary, we may cut ourselves off from the very
people who can teach us much about how to thrive in ministry.
Bottom line: We forget how to do ministry effectively. This type
of amnesia is the most common malady that I see in local
churches.

It Takes More Than Moses

The most obvious solution to such amnesia would, at first
glance, seem to be for New Harmony to find a superleader who
can, like Moses, lead us against all odds to the promised land (a
vague vision that may vary widely depending upon whom you ask
in a particular church). We are talking here about staking the
hope of our drifting and technologically befuddled congregation
in the discovery and rise of a great pastor-leader who will, by the
sheer power of his or her wisdom and charisma, lead us from the

present wilderness into a brave new future of ministry effectiveness and community relevance. This is mistake number one.

It is difficult to serve on a pastor search committee for a stagnated or declining congregation and not find ourselves wooed by
the romantic hope that the pastor candidate we discover and call
will, in fact, be *the one*: a new Moses, whose leadership will turn
our church around. Of course, this is a wistful and unlikely wish.
On the Monday after the new pastor's first sermon, we will still
be exactly the same group of people, with almost all of the same
constraints we faced before. This fantasy is not unlike a man or
woman rebounding from a second marriage into a hyperactive
dating frenzy in search of *the one* who can wipe away the brokenness and disappointment of the previous two decades.

My observation of pastor (and staff) search committees is that
two opposing forces often counteract each other in the search
process. On one hand, we desire a miracle worker. And on the
other hand, as we stack the candidates against one another, most
of our search committees gravitate away from the more creative,
out-of-the-box leader candidates whose resumes come across our
conference tables. In the end, most search committees err on the
side of choosing persons who are local, persons who have trained
at familiar institutions, or persons whose native instincts and key
skills represent strong continuity with the past as opposed to the
ability to help the congregation create a new future. Search committees are notorious for taking the safe bet, choosing the leader
least likely to rock the status quo enough to affect significantly
our congregational effectiveness. In this way, the would-be Moses
is usually spared the grief of having to wrestle us into the twenty-
first century. Occasionally, of course, progressive voices win out
in the search process, and Reverend Moses gets the job. But then
almost as often, Moses' honeymoon ends quickly and in bitter
conflict over the changes he or she is seeking to bring. I work
with the would-be Reverend Moses on a regular basis. I hear the
pain of resistance that he or she encounters, and I hear about the
hell that family members endure. I have seen more than one
Moses leave, not simply the particular churches they are serving,
but pastoral ministry altogether, beaten and exhausted from the

conflict. After a couple of years trying to push constructive change at New Harmony, *tending secular sheep* in the desert begins to look appealing.

Granted, New Harmony needs bold leadership and, almost certainly, will not experience renewal without a very bold, tenacious leader who is unwilling to take *no* for an answer to the vision in his or her heart. However, it takes more than just getting a bold leader in place. For this reason, wise churches surround their bold new leaders with a support team of lay leaders who forge a coalition. Often, this circle of leaders travels together to a great big church such as Calvary to learn the tricks of effective ministry in the twenty-first century. Mistake number two.

Neither Does the Healing Begin at Saddleback

You see, even if we pass on the temptation to look for healing of our church's ineffectiveness through the discovery of a super-leader, we may fall for yet another tempting pig path in which we invest far too much hope. (A *pig path* is a narrow *path to nowhere* that veers off the main trail, with the false hint that it may actually take us somewhere.) This second false path to renewal is to invest the hope of our church's future in partnership with a teaching church such as Calvary, so as to relearn some necessary proficiencies for ministry, proficiencies ranging from effective Sunday morning children's ministry to more effective communication habits in worship. This idea makes more sense than simply hoping for a miracle worker. And yet, this also proves to be a false path, in short time.

You see, a lot of water has gone under the bridge in the last forty years. Neither Calvary nor New Harmony is anything like what they were back then. The accumulated years, the accumulated effects of choices made, the accumulated effect of the people who have joined (and those who have left)—these accumulated effects add together to produce two churches today that have remarkable and profound differences in what "church" means to their respective members and what habits of church life

115

are most highly valued.

Besides this, Calvary is now just so big that many of New Harmony's leaders would likely become overwhelmed if they sought to make Calvary a pattern for their own ministry in the years ahead. Remove Calvary from the equation and leave a blank. Then insert the following into the blank: Saddleback Church, Willow Creek Church, or North Point Community Church. New Harmonys everywhere regularly send a party of scouts to such megachurches to learn "how to do it," so they can come back home and fix New Harmony. But, for the average New Harmony Church in the world, using such megachurches as the model of the way things should be is unproductive. The differences in language, values, organizational life, and even community context can be so enormous that many of the people at New Harmony, who might otherwise be a part of a change process, will panic, dig in their heels, and align themselves with the two or three controlling families who want to protect the status quo. For such a church, who has tried "Saddlebacking," everything they do with *purpose-drivenness* to the point that they have scared many of their best leaders to death, often the result is disaster. The product of such a relationship with a giant teaching church may be that New Harmony (a) runs off its pastor and (b) retrenches into old habits even more stubbornly than before. Rather than finding healing from amnesia, the pathology simply deepens.

The Teaching Congregation

Even though Saddleback and Willow Creek are probably not the answer, the fact remains that healing of New Harmony will more likely come about if the church's leaders immerse themselves in the culture of another congregation, whose habits of life and skills of ministry are appropriate for New Harmony. In review, both *hoping for Moses* and *copycatting the megachurch* are wrong moves. Nonetheless, we still need a bold leader at New

Harmony, and we still need to find a congregation (or two) that can mentor New Harmony.

This teaching church, which could be so helpful to New Harmony, probably does not have a world-renowned pastor. Neither does it have six thousand members or a national leadership seminar with a slick brochure. But almost certainly there *is* a church out there that can help New Harmony. This church may not have ever even considered the possibility of becoming a teaching congregation. This church could help New Harmony rediscover helpful habits of ministry effectiveness in a new age. *The marks of this potential teaching church* are as follows. The more of these statements that are true, the more promising the possibilities.

- The potential teaching church was either *stagnant or in decline within the past decade, but turned around,* most likely due to leader initiative rather than to a favorable change in community demographics.
- The potential teaching church works within a *similar cultural setting* to the community of the church that it would mentor. (If our goal is movement toward a community-driven ministry, then similarity of community contexts is more important than similarity of congregational cultures. There may still be major differences between the community cultures, but enough overlap of issues that the learning church senses relevance.)
- The potential teaching church *either has been similar in size to the learning church* in the past decade *or is now no larger than two times the size of the learning church* (in the number of weekly participants). If either of these conditions is present, there will be a mutual, often unspoken, understanding of *how things work* in the congregational life of churches this size.
- *The turnaround pastor is still in leadership.* We are talking about the leader who was at the helm during the years when congregational values and behaviors

117

shifted and the years of stagnancy or decline came to an end. If this key pastoral leader is no longer present, then it is extremely important that the growth of the teaching church's ministry has continued under the present pastor's leadership.

- There is *a good chemistry between the pastors* of both the teaching church and the mentored church. Or, at the very least, the pastor of the learning congregation has respect for the pastor of the teaching congregation.

- Finally, there *may* be a *big-cheese layperson in the teaching congregation who saw the light*. In the world of Jewish synagogues, this kind of person is sometimes called a *macher*. This is a Yiddish word meaning "a mover and a shaker," usually a big benefactor financially, possibly the matriarch or patriarch of one of the leading families in the church. This person may have resisted the changes of a few years back but now sees the wisdom of those changes. This person probably still enjoys being in charge in all of life's arenas; indeed he or she may still try to call many of the shots at the teaching church. But, *this person's heart is profoundly right with God*. This person's passion for the community causes him or her now to run offense rather than defense when it comes to the church's mission. In many cases, most of the *machers* may have dropped out of church life during the season of turnaround. But where one or two hung in there and embraced the change, they can be incredibly helpful in convincing the leaders of the would-be learning church about both the urgency of change and the joy that will come from it.

In the case of New Harmony, a helpful partner and mentor turned out to be the Saint Mark United Methodist Church, a church on the outskirts of another midsized Southern city, about one hundred miles from Big Creek. Saint Mark is a church of 220 in Sunday attendance that has been steadily growing again for the last six years. Saint Mark is far from perfect. Yet it has two or three really positive habits of church life that have marked it during this recent renaissance, behaviors that are well within the reach of New Harmony. By sending delegations to worship with Saint Mark on Sunday and to dialogue with the leadership (*both* in plenary sessions, in which Saint Mark leaders—clergy and lay—speak on various topics to the leader team from New Harmony *and* in one-on-one dialogue between leaders from Saint Mark and New Harmony), a relationship begins. This relationship may be deepened through shared mission trips, shared youth trips, shared leadership visioning retreats, and so on. The possibilities are endless. In short, the more time the two churches spend together interacting, the more opportunity we have for the attitudes and positive culture of Saint Mark to infect New Harmony. One of the real blessings in this relationship for New Harmony was the discovery that in a couple of areas, they were actually ahead of Saint Mark in ministry development. This was a real encouragement to the New Harmony leaders and a sign that they were partnering with a church that was not entirely out of their league.

The Learning Congregation

Just as some churches enjoy just enough ministry success that they are ready and able to teach other congregations, there are still other churches that are ready and open to learn. Not every church is called to be a teaching congregation. But I have yet to discover a church that is not called to be a learning congregation. In fact, the best teaching congregations are also places in which the leadership has an incessant thirst for learning as well. Churches (and people) who have ceased learning have begun dying. Perhaps the major constraint to New Harmony's development over the past decades has been that the church has not been in the habit of regularly and steadily learning and relearning what it takes to be an effective church.

The marks of potential learning congregations are as follows. The more of these conditions that are present in a congregation's life, the more likely it is that the congregation can incorporate new skills and competencies into its ministry.

- *The pastor of the learning church is hungry to learn* new skills *and grateful for the opportunity* to be mentored by a pastor who is a few years ahead on a similar leadership journey. This pastor is also able to incorporate the learning into effective leadership.
- *A core of key leaders* (not all key leaders, simply a strong core) in the learning church is *enthusiastic about the partnership* with the teaching church and is open to any positive lessons that can be learned.
- *The learning church's leadership team is spiritually ready* to enter the land God desires to give it. Prayer and fasting have occurred. Some new blood has been shifted into leadership in preparation for the future. There is a sense of expectancy on the part of several leaders that something good is about to happen; they are just not sure what.
- *The leaders of the learning church understand and agree that God desires to do a new thing at their church,* not simply a rerun of what happened long ago at their church or a rerun of what happened more recently at the church that is mentoring them. They will borrow and copy from other churches, but they will also adjust and adapt ideas to their own setting. The end result will be unique.
- *The learning church is marked by playfulness.* The leadership team is serious about learning new skills and doing great things, but they don't take themselves too seriously. They know how to enjoy life together, how to laugh, how to have fun, how to accept one another in their imperfections. They will try several things that don't work well at first; yet they will resist the temptation to panic and point fingers. Rather, they will smile

and discover the humor in the situation. A playful church is more ready to try again and again, until they achieve whatever it is they are trying to do. And they have fun trying. Having fun is important. Because, so long as we are having fun, we are less likely to give up. So long as we can laugh at ourselves, the anxious ones among us are invited to laugh with us. And, please remember, the anxious ones will be the first to subvert the changes we are trying to make, once we get too serious.

A church does not have to be in a formal relationship to a teaching church in order to be a learning church. However, in the case of New Harmony, the more intentional we can make this relationship with an appropriately matched teaching church, the better.

As New Harmony's ministry grows and thrives, they may remain in a close friendship with Saint Mark, their teaching church. The formal relationship will come to an end. In fact, it is good to spell out an ending date for such a relationship up front. In a few years, New Harmony, itself, may be ready to mentor other congregations. They may partner with or study still other congregations. There may even be a point in time they choose to take a group of scouts to Saddleback to discover principles that are appropriately transferable to New Harmony. For everything there is a season. But a church will benefit more from association with a megachurch when that church has already established positive momentum and accumulated two or three winning seasons under its belt.

The Boutique Down the Street from Walmart Supercenter

In the process of their relationship with Saint Mark, the leaders at New Harmony discovered that their mission was not really to compete with Calvary, at least not directly. Calvary had grown to be more than thirty times the size of New Harmony. There was little chance that New Harmony could wow people the way Calvary wows them. But New Harmony can still wow people, with a different kind of wow.

In recent years, Lyle Schaller has made much of the idea that the twenty-first century belongs primarily to two kinds of congregations—very large congregations and intimate congregations. Schaller is a sociologist and recognizes that trends in the world of organized religion often mirror trends elsewhere in organized society, particularly in the economy. If you look at any commercial center in most cities today, you will see a few very large stores surrounded by a bunch of small stores, mega-stores and boutiques. People like both. People need both. Early in their relationship to Saint Mark, the leaders at New Harmony recognized that they were a boutique.

The boutique often specializes in a few things rather than many. They sometimes (though not always) draw from a more narrow range of customers. Whatever it is the boutique special-izes in, they do it very, very well. When we shop in boutiques we are looking for something different from when we go to Walmart Supercenter.

At a boutique, we expect to be noticed; we expect more inter-action with the store personnel. In fact, if we shop in a boutique often, we may learn the name of the store personnel and they learn our name. We may expect a customized product or service, the nature of which is determined in consultation with store per-sonnel. We may expect a cozy and comfortable ambiance. We may simply want to spare ourselves a mile-long walk to the back of the big store to pick up what we can find ten steps into the boutique, albeit at a slightly higher price. With respect to the particular type of merchandise that the boutique sells, the choices are often greater at the boutique. When you don't try to offer a little of everything, you are able to offer more variety of *some* things.

New Harmony is at an advantage over Calvary in all of the above ways. It is easier for them to learn the names of newcom-ers on their first Sunday. It is easier for them to miss those same newcomers on the first Sunday they are absent and a more man-ageable task to pick up the phone and call them. It is easier for

New Harmony to establish an atmosphere that is cozy and comfortable. There is a pleasant down-to-earthness and unpackaged quality about New Harmony that comes naturally. If Calvary has that quality also, they have to work much harder at it. Almost no one walks into New Harmony expecting the polish of public presentation that they would expect at Calvary. This is not a license for New Harmony to be sloppy, simply a reminder that they can be themselves. Authenticity, coupled with a spirit of hospitality and excellence, goes a long, long way.

Because the sense of intimacy at New Harmony is largely defined in contrast to the giant church down the street, New Harmony could double or even triple in size without losing this contrast, especially if it offers multiple worship services. Just because a church is a boutique does not mean it should try to force all types of people into one cozy worship hour. Boutiques need to be even more customer oriented than big-box superstores. The boutique church often needs to offer worship options even more urgently than the Walmart Supercenter church. Especially in a church that has embraced a 1939 hymnal, it is important that we create an alternative worship service. We may choose to blend a little of this or that in all of our services; we may define a range of style within which we will operate. The decision to try to serve everybody in one service works well occasionally. However, if that strategy is not enabling a church to break through effectively to reach a certain group, then it should be reconsidered. In a multiple service scenario at New Harmony, we might have five services per week, with two of them running thirty or less in attendance, but each meeting the needs of a certain constituency.

The two main reasons that a small church often resists multiple worship services is (a) because the building is too large already without further dividing the crowd and (b) because we want to know everyone. In the first case, we are allowing the size of the sanctuary to drive us, and that is never a wise thing. Sanctuaries serve churches, not vice versa. In the second case, we overlook the facts that one size does not fit all *and* that by means of multiple services, our church can grow while retaining its boutique feel in worship.

Healed of Amnesia, New Harmony Can Be Lots of Fun!

Once New Harmony breaks out of its slumber and stagnancy, it can become even more fun than the big party that goes on seven days a week down the street. In fact, some of its most promising potential participants will be people who fell through the cracks down at Calvary or who became bored with the show. I would even go so far as to say that if the leaders at New Harmony would go to the leaders of Calvary and ask for the names of their inactive members and visitors, there is more than a chance that Calvary will give New Harmony the names and say, "Go get 'em if you can." It never hurts to ask, if we ask in the right spirit. It may help if New Harmony comes to the table with their own tiny list of inactives in hand to trade as a gesture of thank-you to Calvary.

If New Harmony is simply *ready* to love the people who come through its doors, I can almost guarantee that it will begin to pick up Calvary strays. There is almost no way that Calvary can enjoy and celebrate the gift of each new person who comes through its doors as effectively as New Harmony, if indeed New Harmony is ready to love the folk God sends them. Coming to a church like New Harmony can approach the feeling that the prodigal son had when Dad commissioned the big barbeque! Calvary, because of its sheer size, has to work much harder to create the same feeling in its newcomers.

One of the differences between a church of over eight hundred in attendance and a church of under two hundred is that the latter will be less staff-led in its various ministries. Technically, if large-church staff members understand and practice their proper roles, there should be equal opportunities for lay leadership in ministry at all sizes of congregations. In reality, however, most large churches are staff-dominated, especially in their core ministries. At New Harmony, lay leaders know that if they don't do it, there is not a staff member to see to it someone else does. At New Harmony, I know that if I don't do it, it may well not get done. That fact alone is a great motivator for many people and lends a sense of significance to the ministry task at hand, whatever it may be.

The bottom line is that anytime we sense that we are a part of something that God is doing, the energy of the enterprise begins to infect us positively, and we begin to have fun! Being a part of the renewal of a church and witnessing and sharing in its transformation from a tired church into a feisty outreaching body, there is nothing in all the world more fun than that!

Study Questions

1. Is your church a boutique, a Walmart Supercenter, or something else yet? Why do you say this?

2. If you are a boutique, have you discovered the fun of offering more than one option of worship within the particular flavor and focus of your church? If so, what has been the result? If not, why not?

3. Is there a group of people vocally (or quietly) opposed to the church reaching out and fulfilling the Great Commission? What group in your church is going to stand up to them? Will you be a part of that group who stands up to the naysayers? Would you be willing to adopt a particular naysayer, with whom you have a relationship, and pray for him or her and possibly speak to him or her about the needed changes?

4. How would you classify how well your church connects with and disciples certain population groups in your community? Poor, fair, good, excellent, world-class? What group or groups are you currently reaching? (Note: The question is not what people are we serving who have been with us for several years, but who are we newly reaching.)

5. If there is a population group with which your church is connecting, what is it that you do or that you offer in ministry that is different from what churches

around you are doing, which is not reaching these same people? Might your church mentor another church in how to minister effectively to these folks?

6. Is there a group that you wish your church would do a better job of reaching? What group would this be? What kinds of ministry skills are needed for effectiveness with this group?

7. If you know of a church that is currently reaching new people, can you describe this church's style, values, and special emphases? Do you think this church could be a possible teaching congregation for your church? Why or why not? Look again at the traits of a learning congregation on pages 119-21 and examine your church in the light of each. Where do you see the need for improvement? Can you agree on two specific steps that can be put into action immediately?

CHAPTER 6

HEALING SPIRITUAL AMNESIA IN YOUR CHURCH

"Wake up, O sleeper, rise from the dead, and Christ will shine on you." Ephesians 5:14 NIV

Reviewing the Characters

This book has been built around several key characters. These key characters are not individuals, but congregations. Most of these congregations are fictional. Except those noted below, these churches exist entirely in my imagination. They are composites of many congregations in many places. Any resemblance between one of these congregations and the place you call your spiritual home is accidental, at least on my part. However, I would hope that at least one or two of these churches remind you of your own church. Let's review our characters:

- **Trinity Church** (chapter 2): The church that has become fuzzy in terms of its core beliefs about Jesus Christ.
- **Grace Church** (chapter 2): The church that never forgot who Jesus is, but whose members were taken aback by the explosive renewal that suddenly occurred at the sleepy church (Trinity Church) across the street.
- **Bethany Church** (chapter 3): The church that has become casual of heart, where people spend only a token amount of time together seeking God.
- **The Bible study woman, the young convert, and the registered nurse** (chapter 4): The church that is too preoccupied with other concerns truly to see either the needs or the gifts of the people around them.
- **The two good Samaritans** (chapter 4): The church that, regardless of theological slant, still understands that there is no substitute for hands-on *caring* for God's precious children all around us.
- **Government Street Church** (a real-life congregation, in chapter 4): The church that has decided, against all odds, to get back in the business of serving its community.
- **Calvary Church** (chapter 5): The church that has stayed on the cutting edge of relevancy and effectiveness with a changing community and a changing culture. Calvary is a church that can mentor others. However, even though Calvary has excelled at the mechanics of ministry within a certain demographic, it can still fall into amnesia in other areas. Just because a church is big and slick does not mean it is remembering the disciplines of personal spiritual development or that it is remembering the suffering of its neighbors.

- **New Harmony Church** (chapter 5): The church that has fallen behind the times and is now both isolated from its community and unskilled in ways to make up for lost time. There may be more people from New Harmony who pick up this book than from any other type of church. There are thousands of New Harmonies out there.

Make a note of the church or churches that remind you of your own congregation, and write down why you see the connection. Go back to the chapter that contained the church you have identified with, and review if a particular path to that church's healing was identified in that chapter or in another.

Armed with this information, you have now accomplished two things: (1) You have identified a core issue in your congregation, and (2) you have at least an idea of how a church such as yours might find its memory healed. In every case, the healing of spiritual amnesia is largely beyond human control. There is no foolproof therapy, no road maps guaranteeing to deliver us in a certain place. However, in most cases, the amnesia is a symptom and result of another kind of wound or stress. Healing will thus need to relate to the particular wound that may have precipitated the amnesia.

At Trinity, a convergence of special events that no one but God could have planned provided the spark for the church's healing. At Bethany, my prescription was the creation of a network of cell groups. And yet, cell group systems often do not form easily in established congregations. They require enormous commitment and focus on the part of church leadership; and to succeed, they require God's touch and blessing. Again, we can't program God's blessing. With respect to the amnesia that causes us to forget our neighbors, the road to health is illustrated by Government Street Church, a church that dares to believe God is giving it a future in ministry to its neighbors, even though both the odds against it and the future obstacles are enormous. With God, and only with God, are such things possible as the renewal of an old downtown church dwindled to a handful of octogenarians, isolated from the new cultures of the city. At New Harmony, the help of a sister congregation was helpful in the church's healing. But still, for healing truly to come to New Harmony, there must be healing from the obsession with the past and the hostage-taking tactics of certain controllers in lay leadership. Again, these are God-sized obstacles.

Healing Is, by Definition, a God-thing

There are things we do, and then there is what God does. Without the God part, healing cannot occur. Any wise physician understands this like he or she understands breathing. This is why the work of healing should always be bathed in prayer. This is true at the hospital, where we seek to heal individuals, and equally true at the church, where we seek to heal both individuals and whole communities. Too often, prayer is an afterthought, something we do in perfunctory ways out of polite respect for God. Prayer should reflect an utter dependency upon God.

Healing was absolutely at the core of Jesus' ministry. Jesus' ministry actually hinged on a synergy between two key tasks: teaching and healing. The healing demonstrated the truths contained in his stories and confirmed the moral authority in the words he shared. The stories interpreted the healing. If Jesus had been merely a good teacher or merely a healer, his life story would have been lost to us. It was the combination of amazing healing and profound teaching that caused Jesus to catch the widespread attention of first-century Palestinian society and of communities around the world in our century.

The healing was always a sign that God was present in Jesus Christ. Jesus depended upon God for the power to heal. *Even Jesus knew better than to try healing on his own.*

Pastor and church leadership teams who may be contemplating the task of healing their church's spiritual amnesia had best recognize that they work with God in their leadership and that, short of getting God in the equation, all their human efforts will add up to very little. Jesus taught us that often we do not have, because we do not ask. It is clear that God desires the revitalization of Christian congregations. So it is probably not God's will that your church fail in its mission or die on the vine. Probably not. It *is* conceivable that God could desire that one congregation fade and die so that another can rise, especially if the first congregation is stubbornly resistant to the changes necessary to make them effective in their ministry. In most cases, however, if we offer our churches to God in prayer and ask for God's hand of healing to lead us in awakening a people from their spiritual amnesia, we can expect God will answer our prayer in the affirmative and will move to do a mighty thing.

So, regardless of the specific healing therapy or strategy we choose, prayer is absolutely foundational! With God, all things are possible for any church, no matter what shape it may be in today. Without God, all kinds of things can become insurmountable limitations. When we remember this reality, we are freed to focus on the possibilities and to look beyond the apparent limitations.

Tending to Old Wounds

On the one hand, we may discover that old wounds need direct attention before we attempt to begin dreaming with God. If key leaders, such as the pastor and several other new leaders, were not present in the life of the congregation when various stresses occurred or have already worked through such experiences personally, they may feel ready to start visioning immediately. In this case, they are free to dream with God and then to tend to the wounds that block others in the church from seeing what they see and from coming with them where God is leading.

If, on the other hand, the whole system has been affected by the amnesia, then the fog may need to lift a bit before we will be free to dream big dreams with God. In this case, we may need to begin by tending to the wounds and the stresses that have contributed to the amnesia.

Again, prayer is the key. So we will begin by asking God to direct us to the sources of pain and stress that have contributed to our present inertia. This prayerful search needs to happen both within the group setting and within the private lives of individuals in the group.

A group of church leaders could begin by reading this book together and sharing their thoughts, their feelings, and relevant memories together. This book is built around some of the most common types of amnesia that I see in churches. It may help a group of leaders become clear that something is not quite right and get the group thinking about and remembering things that they have not thought about recently, if ever. This thinking and praying can continue away from the church, between the times that the group meets.

As I examine case studies of individuals who recovered from amnesia, I am struck by how often the memories came back when they were away from a therapist's office. Most often it was when they were at home, when they were alone or with a friend or family member. This makes sense to me. A therapist's office can at times be a much more stressful environment than a home setting. This isn't because therapists are a scary group of people, but because we may come to the therapist's office focusing on scary things in our lives. When we go home, when we get by ourselves, most of us relax. There appears to be some correlation between relaxing and recovering memory. In fact, sometimes, the first line of therapy is to give an amnesiac patient some kind of chemical relaxant to get him or her to relax and start talking and, once they are fully sober, to continue the conversation. Hypnosis may be administered along the same line of reasoning.

So, if we are part of a church that is seeking to discover what it is that has frozen us in time, we may need some time away from the church to ponder the question alone with God or in the quiet company of a trusted friend who is not a member of our church. We may also choose to do some things with fellow church members that help us relax. A group that is capable of both laughing together and praying together can accomplish much together!

As we experience "aha!" moments in our time apart from the group, we can come back and share our thoughts and discoveries with group members. This then helps the others begin remembering important things.

The First Group to Read This Book

In the final preparation of this manuscript, I invited a group of leaders from a reasonably healthy church near my home to read the first five chapters of this book and meet regularly over the course of a month, discussing their church's ministry in light of what they read. Between ten and twelve persons gathered each time we met. Together, we discovered some things that cast light on a few of the significant ministry frontiers for their church.

In the very first session, the group identified the second amnesia (forgetting the spiritual disciplines) as the primary issue that held their church back from its potential. This was a church with an excellent outreach program and community ministry, a church whose growing edge was to find ways of taking folks deeper as disciples of Jesus Christ. However, in future sessions, they discovered some significant needs for growth in each of the other areas.

Most group members shared experiences from other churches and from this particular church in years prior to the present era. In most cases, the comparisons cast a positive light on the present situation in their church. They observed how their church, in recent years, had become more effective in helping people develop relationships with Jesus Christ. They shared horror stories from here and there of churches that were closed to neighbors or were hopelessly reliving yesterday.

On the second night, as they explored chapter 2, one man observed that not everyone has a spiritual *wow* experience of meeting Jesus. But when they began sharing the particular experiences in *their* lives that were most significant in terms of developing their relationship with Jesus, all eyes in the room were suddenly opened. Two of our group had been caught on a small sailboat in the Caribbean during a hurricane, praying constantly for God to spare their lives from what seemed imminent death. Two others recounted near-death moments as patients in an emergency room, one who came so close to death that she literally recalled floating above the scene and watching the people work on her. Another shared how her son was missing for days and was presumed dead after his abandoned truck was found. (He was later found alive!) In each case, they had encountered the living Christ in these incredibly traumatic moments. In each case, they found inexplicable peace. And in each case, they look back to these events, which many people might consider *nightmare* moments, as the *defining* moments of their relationship to God. None of the group members had ever heard these remarkable stories from one another. Had I added my own experience to the mix, there would have been six such stories that night, involving half the group! The great *aha!* moment was how many *wow* experiences were hidden in a typical gathering of church leaders, experiences they had never shared before with one another. And even those in the room who may have felt their spiritual journey was a bit mild in comparison were blessed by discovering how God had worked in the lives of the ordinary, down-to-earth people around them.

A great lesson emerged from the discussion of chapter 2: There are some stories buried in our hearts that we need to be sharing with one another and with the world beyond the church's walls. Perhaps the greatest result that could come to a group exploring chapter 2 would be to begin sharing with one another the moments in life when they discovered the living Christ or the pivotal moments that have moved them forward in their relationship to Christ. Such sharing could go a long way toward lifting the amnesia about Jesus that plagues so many Christian communities.

As the discussion moved to chapter 3, several people shared recent experiences with small groups in this particular church. Though only a small fraction of the total membership had been involved in such groups to date, the consensus was that such groups were the key to this church's future. Had there not been some people present who had firsthand experience with the value of small groups, this might have been a more difficult conversation.

One group member made the point that we don't have time to spend hours in our kitchens cooking in the present era, but still we eat. The corollary idea was that we also do not have the amount of time to devote to church that we once had, but still we grow spiritually. Another group member, picking up on the food metaphor, observed that the latest news about American nutrition, in fact, reveals that fast food is killing us. The corollary idea here is that our spiritual health is damaged when we try to eat on the run, spiritually. Still another observed that at the rate that life sped up over the past century, and at the rate that our time spent in spiritual things diminished, we will all be unchurched by the year 2100. She posed the question, "What will David IV's great-grandson discover when he ventures into the same closet a hundred years from now?" She was asking a good question.

One woman observed, "We have a lot of new believers here. In many cases, they have not *forgotten* the disciplines of the Christian life; they just haven't learned them yet." She proceeded to ask, "So is this amnesia? How can I forget what I've never known to begin with?" My response was this: No, those individuals did not have amnesia. But the church (considered collectively), which has been affected by scores of new seekers and new believers in a relatively short period, has experienced a relative loss of memory of the habits and disciplines that are key to Christian health and growth. The church had welcomed new disciples on board, but the church had not been adequately assertive in getting those young disciples into groups, experiences, and relationships that would move them forward spiritually. The longer they waited to do so, the more likely these new believers would settle for being simply observers and spiritual consumers, contented with a one-hour-a-week commitment. In short time, the church as a whole would no longer remember the value of spending time in the disciplines of learning, sharing, praying, serving, and growing. In this case, the precipitating stressor would have been not a bad stress, but a good stress: the introduction of a large number of new Christians into the system all at once without an adequate plan in place to help them get grounded in the habits of a Christian life.

It became apparent that this church faced a critical need for a well-oiled small-group system and method of mentoring and assimilating newcomers. Questions about when to build the next unit or when to have the next capital fund campaign faded to a distant second in urgency.

This church prided itself on strong awareness of neighbor's needs and orientation to meeting those needs. In fact, they could be considered cutting edge in certain respects. Nonetheless, as the group began exploring chapters 4 and 5, they discovered some important opportunities for growth and development.

First, they realized that as a suburban church, they served a more homogeneous community than did many congregations. A couple of individuals remarked that the monotone racial color of their part of town had taken some getting used to after they had previously lived in communities with more demographic diversity. Second, they began to see that their church was, racially speaking, really no different from the church in chapter 3 with the locked doors and buzzers. (This was a great discovery!) Despite relating well to the immediate neighbors, the church was still somewhat isolated as a part of the larger community of peoples in their metro area. This led me to ask the group, "Where does your church's neighborhood end? Does it stop several miles away where geographic boundaries and railroad tracks mark a shift in racial and socioeconomic categories, or should it extend beyond such boundaries?" Several group members expressed a desire for more cross-cultural and cross-racial opportunities in terms of worship leadership and partnering with congregations across town that serve different people groups. Finally, one woman took a stab at answering my question directly. She said, "Our neighborhood stops where our strength gives out." I felt this statement revealed powerful insight. She explained that a congregation should extend as far as it has the energy, the gifts, and the people power to go. This conversation revealed to me that even in a church that does not suffer from profound amnesia about its immediate neighbors, *there is always an opportunity to grow in connection with others*, as we open our eyes.

The group concluded with four clear action issues on the table, which I would rank in the following order of urgency: (1) the need to move quickly to develop and grow their small-group network, (2) the need to talk to and learn from churches in their region that excelled in ministry to twenty-something adults, (3) the need to strengthen their ministry partnership with people and churches serving different people groups, and (4) the need to further highlight the faith stories of ordinary people in their worship services. Each of these matters could now be pursued deliberately, and prayerfully, as they depend upon God to open the doors, soften certain hearts, and reveal the way.

The Danger of Obsessing over Bricks and Mortar

As a congregational developer, I regularly go in and meet with leaders of congregations, listen, ask appropriate questions, and offer a set of recommendations. Very often such leadership summits are called because of issues relating to buildings, money, or significant changes in participation levels. These are each important issues. However, if in this quest for direction, we limit our concern to bottom-line business issues, we may stabilize our church as a business and still not help our church in terms of its core mission and health. Ultimately, churches are not built of bricks and mortar: They are built of holy memories and living relationships.

This book is written for leaders of local churches: for pastors, board members, staff members, interventionists, leadership team members, planning committee members, trustees, elders, deacons, and any others who love their church and want to lend their energy to helping their church thrive and fulfill its God-given purposes. This book is designed to shift our focus away from the bricks-and-mortar concerns that boards and leadership teams spend most of their time on. It is a book that seeks to invite *a gentle yet pointed conversation* among the leaders of a congregation around the most important issues of their common life. Out of such a conversation, some very urgent issues will emerge. As groups of leaders wrestle with and pray through these issues, conflicts *may* arise, but consensus *will* usually emerge. Neglected matters of importance will be talked about again. Mission statements will be honed. Fuzzy issues will become sharper.

In the wake of this process, we are then much more ready to talk about buildings and money and institutional strategy. Not only will better buildings get built, but better churches will be built. If, however, we as leaders *cut to the chase* and just talk church business with one another, we will short-circuit the important task of reflecting on who we are in relation to Jesus, in relation to the disciplines, in relation to our neighbors, and in relation to our habits and strategies.

Whenever I have worked with churches that resisted and rebelled against obvious and simple ministry coaching, I have often discovered *in hindsight* a church mired in underground conflict. In such cases, I have also *always* discovered a church suffering from debilitating amnesia. In those cases, it would be much better for the pastor and leaders first to work through the issues in this book and only then to tackle matters of strategy and planning.

Opening Up to God's Future

Reading the book may help bring consensus of diagnosis to our leaders, but there is no magic in these pages. This book will not heal a church. In praying for our church's healing, we may wish to begin by asking God to place within us the vision we need to have. Too often, we calculate, we plan, and we dream dreams on our own and then pray for God to bless what we've come up with. Some of the problems that arise from the practice of simply tacking prayer onto our visioning/planning process are as follows:

- We do not invite God into the formation of our plans.
- We may dream too small.
- Our own egos can skew the vision from what God wants it to be.
- We continue to run scared of limitations and earthly constraints, rather than face them head-on and conquer them.

When we invite God into the process of charting our church's course, both up-front and throughout the process, we can expect the following things to happen:

- Our vision becomes more kingdom oriented and less institutional (more about doing God's mission and less about building a particular organization or a particular facility).
- We become more flexible and nimble, able to adjust to change more easily.
- We no longer feel overwhelmed by an *audacious* plan, because we know that God is in it.
- Miracles will abound.

The whole discipline of long-range planning (which in the 1980s became strategic planning and in the 1990s, strategic mapping) comes to the church from secular industry. Secular industry does not typically expect divine intervention to be a major component in the unfolding of its future. On the contrary, any church that does not expect divine intervention can hardly be called a church. The church by nature must be open to respond to the utterly unexpected, the things that happen by God's hand, the things that no one could have planned or expected.

The corporate world does not typically contend with incorporating God stuff into its planning. Nonetheless, most companies have still moved away from rigid long-range planning. The main reason for this shift is that they discovered the variables to be continually changing. Almost any five- to ten-year plan is largely obsolete after the first year. The resignation of a key staff member or the cheap and sudden availability of an asset the company needs to buy can make a plan obsolete just hours after the ink is dry.

Long-range plans may be helpful, however, if they at least give us a vision of going *somewhere*, as opposed to sitting still. This is akin to a high school student deciding she wants to be a physician and then sitting down with her school counselor to map a way from here to there. This dream and corresponding plan motivates the student to study hard and to make sacrifices and choices that support her dream. Her friends who lack such concrete personal ambitions may drift more easily and more easily become distracted by the various temptations of youth. But our little dreamer and planner, she stays on track. And then, this same student, once she is in college, comes up against a new reality that she did not anticipate in high school. She may not make the grades to go to medical school. Or she discovers that the actual work of physicians does not really fit her personality and gifts. So her dream changes, and her plan changes. But she can still look back and give thanks that the dream of being a doctor kept her focused and moving forward during some very critical years when many young people lose all focus and direction. It would be tragic if she chose to pursue the doctor path after the point she has learned that another path is more appropriate. Why might she stubbornly cling to a path that doesn't fit with her gifts? She might do this to save face with her parents. Or she might be enamored with the earnings potential. At this point, the long-range plan could become an albatross around her neck.

With churches, as with students, a flexible long-range plan can be a symbol of our future. As long as we understand that it is merely a symbol of where God may be leading us, then it can allow us to make some good decisions now, decisions that move us forward while keeping our long-term options as open as possible. If we view a plan as an exact and binding thing, then we may miss the future that God intends to give us altogether. A plan must be renewed continually as new realities become apparent. And, of course, the renewal process should be bathed in prayer, saturated with openness to what God might reveal.

A Closing Admonition

On April 4, 1742, Oxford student Charles Wesley preached a hair-raising sermon in University Chapel. It was a time and place at which profound amnesia gripped the Church of England. He titled his impetuous youthful diatribe "Awake, Thou that Sleepest." He based it on the words of Ephesians 5:14: "Awake thou that sleepest, and arise from the dead, and Christ shall give thee light" (KJV).

Charles Wesley's brother John may have lent his hand to the sermon's writing, evidenced by the fact that John Wesley placed the sermon as number three in the official collection of his sermons that became the plumb line for Methodist doctrine. Few sermons, let alone student sermons, have ever been as widely distributed as "Awake, Thou that Sleepest."

In this famous message, the Wesley brothers use the metaphor of sleep rather than amnesia. But beyond the metaphor chosen, the reality they address in eighteenth-century England is exactly the same reality we face today: a pervasive cluelessness and detachment from our identity and mission as God's people. The closing words of the sermon make a good end to this book. They are a fitting admonition to us and a prayer to God, all wrapped together.

> My brethren, it is high time for us to awake out of sleep; before "the great trumpet of the Lord be blown," and our land become a field of blood. O may we speedily see the things that make for our peace, before they are hid from our eyes! "Turn thou us, O good Lord, and let thine anger cease from us. O Lord, look down from heaven, behold and visit this vine"; and cause us to know the time of our visitation. "Help us, O God of our salvation, for the glory of thy name; O deliver us, and be merciful to our sins, for thy name's sake." "And so we will not go back from thee: O let us live, and we shall call upon thy name. Turn us again, O Lord God of hosts, show the light of thy countenance, and we shall be whole."

"Now unto him that is able to do exceeding abundantly above all that we can ask or think, according to the power that worketh in us, unto him be glory in the church by Christ Jesus throughout all ages, world without end. Amen."[1]

Note

1. John Wesley, "Awake, Thou That Sleepest," *The Works of John Wesley*, vol. 1, ed. Albert C. Outler (Nashville: Abingdon Press, 1984), 158.